Gardenista

Gardenista

The
Definitive
Guide to
Stylish
Outdoor
Spaces

ARTISAN
NEW YORK

Michelle Slatalla
With the editors of **GARDENISTA**

Edited by JULIE CARLSON
Photographs by MATTHEW WILLIAMS

Contents

Introduction

It started with a phone call. "I have a terrible mint problem," my friend Julie Carlson confided. "Can you come take a look?" We'd known each other for a while: We lived in the same small town in Northern California, our daughters went to school together, I wrote a column for the *New York Times*, and she edited Remodelista. I was used to making house calls.

"I'm on my way over," I said.

The diagnosis was clear: runaway mint. It was merrily growing between the bricks on her terrace. "That's not where I want it," Julie said. She had planted it in a raised bed at least 2 feet away. But the next spring, as if it had taken a bus or something, the herb was sunning itself on the bricks. "Pull it from the cracks and pour boiling water on the roots," I said. "Right away."

Julie made me a cup of mint tea from the deceased and served it up with a big idea. For several years, she and the group of her friends who created Remodelista had been focused on interior design. What if we created a sister site, an online sourcebook to offer guidance on every aspect of exterior design, from landscaping and hardscape materials to outdoor lighting fixtures and the perfect paint color for your front door?

Thus was born Gardenista. For the past four years, we've spent most of our waking hours sleuthing out the best projects, products, and design ideas; we can help you choose the right Japanese pruning shears, fragrant old French roses, and midcentury house numbers.

We believe gardens matter. So does your patio, your porch, your front stoop, or the sunny windowsill outside your apartment window. The proof is everywhere: treating the outdoors as a natural extension of living space makes you happier. Whether your patch of green is perched on a balcony or sprawled across five acres, it's your landscape to personalize.

And that's the challenge. How do you design an outdoor space, from hardscape to plants? How do you find the best last-a-lifetime tools? And where can you source everything you need to furnish your outdoor sanctuary?

This book answers those questions. It is a version of Gardenista you can dog-ear. To collect our favorite projects—from a secret seaside retreat on Cape Cod to an antiquarian's cottage garden in London (complete with church spire)—we traveled around the United States and Europe with the talented photographer Matthew Williams. He captured everything from sweeping views of town house backyards to close-ups of the details that imbue a garden with an unmistakable personality. Use this manual as a go-to resource, whether you want to re-create a planting scheme, choose outdoor furnishings, or install a stylish drainage system (not an oxymoron).

With *Gardenista*, it's our mission to demystify garden design, whether you're planning a complete landscape overhaul or just hoping to corral your renegade mint. It doesn't matter if you're a neophyte or a master gardener: you can do this.

The Gardenista Manifesto

TEN RULES TO LIVE BY

01

Outdoor space is living space,
and should be as carefully
considered as any other room
in your home.

02

Curb appeal counts. The
experience visitors have as they
walk up to your front door
makes them feel at home.

03

Spend on permanence.
Investing in quality hardscape
materials gives your garden
good bones.

04

Plant for the garden you
will have five years from now:
sow seeds, buy small pots, and
trade cuttings. Your patience
will save you lots of money in
the long run.

05

A hedge makes a better
neighbor than a fence.

06

Buy beautiful tools and you will
enjoy using them for a lifetime.

07

Make the garden part of your
daily routine by planting
something you can eat for
dinner (parsley counts).

08

A dash of color, whether from
paint or plants, sets the mood
for an outdoor space.

09

The view from your
bedroom window should
include something that
blooms every spring.

10

Choose personality over
perfection; a little wildness in
the garden is a good thing.

Thirteen Gardens We Love

(AND WHY THEY WORK)

Come through the gate with us to explore thirteen of our favorite gardens of all sizes (in the city, the country, and suburbia), designed by their owners to erase boundaries between life outdoors and in. We'll reveal their design secrets and give you tips on how to use their ideas in your own landscape.

Gardenista Headquarters

After my husband, Josh Quittner, and I bought our Spanish Revival bungalow, we resurrected a previous owner's garden and added modern elements, including a colorful perennials bed inspired by the planting scheme of New York City's High Line Park.

OPPOSITE: My husband and I planted a fast-growing hedge of *Pittosporum tenuifolium* 'Silver Sheen' to provide more privacy than our old picket fence; the small-leafed shrub is dense enough to persuade our papillons, Sticky (at left) and Larry, not to try to escape.

The garden was a mystery when my husband and I first saw the house seven years ago. It looked like something from a particularly grim Grimm's fairy tale: overgrown vines, thorns, the poison sisters (ivy, oak, and sumac), and a threatening teaberry tree that once jumped in front of our car and ripped off the side mirror while I happened to be driving. The real estate agent claimed a previous owner had been a gardener. Was she talking about an owner from the nineteenth century, my husband wondered?

This was not a challenge I could pass up. A gardener all my life (there's some talk of how the surname "Slatalla" was an Ellis Island garbling of a word that means "lettuce farmer" in Polish), I suspected this was a garden worth restoring. The tricky part would be to figure out how to revive the best of the past while creating a modern garden.

Soon after we bought the house, I became the editor of Gardenista, which was a lucky thing for my garden in progress. As I started to make over the garden, I also was thinking about gardens all day at work. I became obsessed with Dutch garden designer Piet Oudolf's painterly landscapes and wanted to create a bold gesture of color to greet visitors.

When we cleared the brush in the front garden, we discovered a charming series of winding paths. Suddenly I could see the garden's structure.

For my homage-to-Oudolf design, the wish list included perennial plants that were drought-resistant (California has water woes), deer-proof (the garden is not fenced), and varying heights to create a rolling swath of color on my gently sloped property. The choices included many plants with purple, yellow, or white flowers (a palette I have always liked), so I limited the planting beds to those colors. I liked the result so much that I eventually extended the color scheme to unify the whole garden (in the backyard, we have a lot of white roses and espaliered olive trees). Up next? I recently learned about an old-fashioned purple lilac bred for our mild climate and think the shrub's perfume might be just the thing to invoke the ghost of that long-ago homeowner who made this garden. I need to find a spot for it.

Illusion of Grandeur

Seen from the vantage of our front porch, a 25-foot-tall dracaena—which decades ago may have been a transplanted houseplant—has grown into a useful focal point for our small garden, drawing the eye inward (and away from the neighbors' house behind it).

Perennial Power

Inspired by Dutch garden designer Piet Oudolf's drought-resistant planting scheme for New York City's High Line Park, I combined perennials in shades of purple, white, and yellow (punctuated by drifts of Mexican feather grass and the silver-green foliage of *Artemisia* 'Powis Castle'). Repeat bloomers that flower from April to October include purple *Salvia nemorosa* 'Caradonna' and *Perovskia atriplicifolia* 'Little Spire', yellow *Achillea millefolium*, and fragrant white heliotrope.

Bonus Room

The front porch plays the role of
open-air mudroom, kitted out with
furnishings designed to withstand
weather: a vintage bench salvaged
from a Brooklyn police station's waiting
room, a woven wood umbrella basket
from Hudson Grace, and IKEA's Portis
hat rack.

Welcome Home

We have our neighbor Richard to thank for our lacy stair rail. One day after he saw us patching the stoop, he came by with an ornately patterned section of rusted iron that a previous owner of our house had found in the cellar and given him to use as a trellis. From that fragment, a blacksmith fabricated a rail that looks as if it's always belonged to the house.

Repeat Bloomers

In the backyard, the garden design relies on repetition: planted against the fence are climbing roses and espaliered olive trees. In front of them bloom fuss-free white Iceberg roses (encouraged by regular deadheading, the disease-resistant variety will bloom from April to October). Clumps of chives send up white puffball flowers in late spring, and in summer the creamy pom-poms of an oak leaf hydrangea (at right) join the party.

Summer Showers
We used basic off-the-shelf plumbing parts to create an instant open-air shower. (We hired a plumber to hook up the pipes.) A simple towel hook and a wall-mounted metal soap dish (also hardware store finds) complete the setup.

01

02

01 Drainage Basics

A bluestone paver serves as a shower mat; water flows into a surrounding bed of bluestone gravel and, from there, percolates into the ground.

02 Every Inch Counts

To convert an unused stretch of our narrow driveway into a kitchen garden, we created a 2-foot-wide garden bed edged with brick and filled it to a depth of 18 inches with soil (every winter we add a layer of compost). From the overgrown garden, we unearthed a vintage birdbath that must have belonged to that long-ago gardener-in-residence; now it's planted with succulents. Creeping fig vines cover the fence with a green curtain, pruned twice a year to prevent it from getting thatchy.

03 Mini Potting Shed

Behind the garage doors is an 18-inch-deep potting shed that reminds me of a Barbie-doll case I had as a child; when you unclasped the lid, you found a whole world of possibility (and many neatly arranged pairs of Barbie shoes) inside. My shed, built by a handyman, has a worktop at just the right height for me. Compartments, shelves, and pegboard hooks corral tools, pots, vases, and garden accessories—and make it easy to see everything at a glance. A pair of lidded Knodd bins from IKEA hold potting soil.

03

Patio Days

The more spots to lounge outdoors the better. In the backyard (at left), French doors connect our kitchen and family room to a sunny bluestone terrace where an extra-deep slatted teak sofa from Terrain encourages afternoon naps. And in a far corner of our front yard (above) is a shady, secret spot with a brick patio just big enough for a table and chairs.

Steal This Look
FOOLPROOF COLOR PALETTE

01
Complementary Colors

To unify disparate spaces, keep both the hardscape and landscape color palettes as simple as possible. Purple, yellow, and white (accentuated by a dash of black) are friends on the color wheel and in life. Look for a purple garden hose like mine (purchased a few years ago from Terrain) at local garden stores.

02
Black Magic

A matte-black finish on a chalkboard planter from West Elm is a foil for the rich colors of a *Calathea*'s leaves, which on the underside are a deep purple. Also nicknamed the zebra plant in honor of its green and white stripes, a *Calathea* is native to tropical climes (bring it indoors if you expect frost) and prefers indirect light.

03
Light Catchers

Clear-glass accessories such as a paperweight and a hanging glass sphere (read more about this natural housefly repellant on page 327) will catch the sun and throw shafts of light around a garden. Like a mirror, a glass surface reflects and emphasizes the greenery in a landscape.

04
Self-Promoter

Aquilegia (commonly known as columbine) is a happy self-sower that likes to reseed itself in a slightly different spot in the garden every year. I let mine grow where it wants; it hasn't picked a bad location yet.

05
Iceberg Roses

Aptly named for the pure-white color of their prolific blooms, these are some of the hardiest repeat-blooming roses available. Iceberg can be trained both as a shrub and a climber, and so far I haven't found a plant it doesn't improve by its proximity. A low, mounded *Polygala fruticosa* 'Petite Butterflies' (at bottom) is a tropical evergreen also known as a sweet pea bush that will bloom year round in USDA growing zones 9 and 10.

An Untamed Secret Garden

Manhattan-based designer and antiques dealer John Derian's old-fashioned Cape Cod garden allows rebellious plants to breach the boundaries of a formal design.

OPPOSITE: Derian runs a seasonal outpost of his eclectic home accessories and dry goods stores from the back of his Provincetown house. Known for his unerring curator's eye, he made himself a household name with his decoupage, which he creates by gluing vintage postcards, handwritten letters, and ephemera to handblown glass. He now sells textiles and garden antiques in addition to his ever-evolving line of decoupage pieces. His private collection includes an antique cast-iron urn-turned-planter (right) that he bought in France. Garden designer Tim Callis drilled a hole for drainage and filled it with *Pelargonium* 'Balcon Pink', which blooms prolifically all summer. Wisteria, *Rosa rugosa*, and raspberry bushes (left) are encouraged to flourish and go wild at the edge of the pea-gravel parking area.

Antiques dealer John Derian's garden is an unapologetically nostalgic backdrop for his throwback summers: charades, afternoons in chaises, candlelit dinner parties. But the unruly garden was a wreck when he first saw it a decade ago, a backdrop for nothing more than the "For Sale" sign on an eighteenth-century sea captain's house. The property's preserved-in-amber quality—from monstrously overgrown hedges to peeling wallpaper—spoke to the Manhattan-based designer, who has a penchant for imposing the style of earlier eras on modern life. At first it looked as if he wouldn't get the house (he was told the property was sold), but two months later, serendipity struck. Back in New York City (where Derian owns an eponymous home accessories store), he googled "Provincetown properties" and up popped the same listing; the sale had fallen through. Should he try again? Derian consulted his friend Tim Callis, a sought-after Cape garden designer based in Wellfleet. "Tim was very busy, but he said, 'If you get the house, I'll do the garden for you,'" Derian says. "So I had to buy the house."

Nearly a decade later, serendipity still rules. Callis's signature style is to create a rigid structure—tall, tightly pruned shrubs and hedges—and then allow the plants within it to get as wild as they like. Although Derian's garden is hemmed in by neighbors on three sides, its deliberately boisterous style (overrun with vines and drifts of lacy flowers) prevents claustrophobia. The out-of-control look is trickier to pull off than it seems. Callis had to impose order on a hodgepodge of outdoor spaces created after nineteenth- and twentieth-century additions made the house sprawl over the property. He designed a series of outdoor rooms for different activities—dining, growing vegetables, parking cars, and growing the flowers Derian snips to make whimsical arrangements (which he loves even more after they begin to die and decay). "They're as beautiful as live plants, just different," says Derian.

Wild Kingdom

Every spring, Callis experiments with wildflowers, sowing seeds directly into the ground alongside pathways. "I go with what does well," he says. On a walkway that runs from the street to the back of the house, low-growing hay-scented ferns are punctuated by bright colors. The trick to getting a wild look, says Callis, is to sow the seeds in full sun, water thoroughly, and, after germination, keep watering the roots regularly through the heat of high summer. "It's not good to fertilize them—just let them go," he says.

Today's Matinee

Four stacking armchairs from Fermob (in Fjord Blue) face a raised bed of edibles and cutting flowers, allowing Derian and his guests to watch the garden grow as if they were watching TV. Plants past their prime are allowed to flower and set seed because, says Callis, "when the lettuces start to bolt, they're just so pretty." Instead of grass, a no-maintenance "lawn" of barn straw surrounds the beds. At the end of the growing season, Callis throws the broken-down straw onto the raised beds and adds manure. "It creates a remarkable compost," he says.

Dinner in Progress

Amid the random sprawl of the edible
garden, Derian "shops" for dinner
ingredients. Whatever's in season,
he harvests: "I eat a lot of kale, like
everybody else in the world now.
But I've been eating it a lot longer."
The birdbath, an antique Derian
acquired in his travels, is "some sort
of ecclesiastical remnant" repurposed
for the garden.

Hiding in Plain Sight
By planting hornbeam in a square—mimicking the shape of the twentieth-century addition to the house—Callis created a private enclosure for a raised-bed garden of vegetables, herbs, and cutting flowers adjacent to the parking area.

01

01 Meadow in Miniature
Alongside the pea gravel parking area, Callis sows wildflower seeds each spring. Blooming against the picket fence is a tangle of shrubs, trees, and flowers, including salmon-colored zinnias.

02 High Season
Seen here tending to tomato plants at the height of summer, Callis sows successive waves of seed in these raised beds—starting in early spring with kale, chard, mesclun, and arugula—throughout the growing months. "It looks very, very random when it comes up; it's kind of fun to see," he says. (The tomatoes are an exception; they are transplanted nursery seedlings.)

03 Just Picked

Derian makes spontaneous bouquets from whatever's in bloom in the garden. Here, a pink echinacea and leggy geraniums in a vintage bottle create an informal arrangement atop the vintage outdoor dining table, which has a galvanized top and metal legs.

04 Outdoor Dining 101

After Derian bought the house, he decided to create a dining area "out of thin air" beneath a second-story porch. Working within the dimensions suggested by an existing brick floor, he had an L-shaped bench built to fit the space. The seat cushions and pillows are covered with textiles and fabrics from his store, including grain sacks and nineteenth-century homespun linens. Vintage onion lamps, many of them converted from kerosene, hang from the ceiling, providing a golden glow at night. A friend made the stools by cutting a nineteenth-century wood beam into lengths at a standard seat height.

An Untamed Secret Garden

Thirteen Gardens We Love

Steal This Look
MISS HAVISHAM'S FLOWERS

01
The Experimental Bouquet

Derian arranges bouquets from the garden, brings them indoors—and then leaves them. For months. "I put them in a vase, and then watch as they just sit there, and shrink down, long after most people would say, 'Oh my God, they're dead,' and get rid of them," he says. "I like the way things age."

02
Embracing the Past

In several rooms, horsehair and seashell plaster walls (original to the 1789 house) are covered with vintage wallpaper, creating an aged effect that Derian heightens with his arrangements of decaying flowers. Here, a dead sunflower and a ripe watermelon, two artifacts of summer, vie for attention on a half-round table in a corner of the dining room.

03
Still Life with Perennials

Snipped from the garden, leaves from a giant hosta fill a bottle. When placed in a simple clear glass container, the stems become a design element as well. The shape of the leaves mimics the four-quadrant pattern on one of the vintage wallpapers that Derian left in place when he renovated the house.

04
Hosta Leaves, Redux

Same hosta leaves, different stage of life. "If these leaves were outdoors, they would disintegrate, but in a vase, they just dry—and become something else," says Derian, who places mirrors strategically, opposite windows, to reflect light.

05
Please Don't Call It a Geranium

Derian, who advocates keeping houseplants in the bedroom for an added pop of color, cultivates pelargoniums (often confused with their cousins, geraniums) gone leggy, a look he achieves by never pinching them back. "All of them are seven years old, and they each get one glass of water a week. That's all," he says. Derian sets the houseplants near windows, where they grow toward the sun on twisted branches.

The Antiquarians at Home

Although Will Fisher and Charlotte Freemantle created their garden from scratch after moving to a central London row house, the lichen-covered fountain, gently worn pathways, and rambunctious jumbled garden beds look as if they have always been there. "The key to success," says Fisher, "is faded grandeur."

OPPOSITE: On sunny mornings, Fisher and Freemantle start the day with coffee and the newspaper in their central London backyard, sitting under a mature apple tree—the only reminder of the previous owners—amid a collection of mix-and-match vintage furnishings they leave outdoors to encourage development of a patina. "Furniture and objects should look as if they've grown roots because they've been in situ for so long," says Fisher.

When antiques dealers Will Fisher and Charlotte Freemantle (cofounders of Jamb Limited on London's Pimlico Road) bought a Georgian row house a decade ago, they knew they wanted their brand-new garden to look as if it had been inherited from a previous century. "It's all about surface and mixing old with new," says Fisher. "In this day and age there is no excuse for new things to be too 'shiny.'" Further, although the couple lives in central London, they wanted the garden to seem as if it belonged to a gracious country house. (Happily, a neighboring church with a tall spire dominates the horizon to suggest a pastoral backdrop.)

The biggest question they faced was how to deal with the long, narrow ribbon of land. After all, a garden 19 feet wide and 120 feet long presents a special design challenge if one wants to avoid the look of a landing strip.

The answer was to divide the elongated rectangle into three distinct "rooms": a cottage garden, a walled garden, and a water garden. The trio of spaces transforms the landscape into a journey, with destinations along the way to a distant focal point: a classical pond that beckons visitors with the sound of running water.

The plantings are layered, particularly along the borders of the backyard, where "blurry edges" make the space appear wider than it is. From years of collecting antique garden ornaments to sell in their shop, the couple had amassed their own trove of urns, planters, and vases that they scattered about the gardens in pairs and trios to reinforce a feeling of haphazard accumulation by generations of gardeners. Says Fisher, "I love creating environments that are entirely new but appear authentic in every way."

Forging a Connection

When Fisher and Freemantle bought their house, the ground-floor kitchen had no access to the backyard garden. "The kitchen had a door leading to a tiny boxed-in patio, which made it very damp and dark," says Fisher. To marry the kitchen to the garden, they doubled the size of the doors and serendipitously found some eighteenth-century Portland stone steps that, "while massively overscaled, were exactly the right length to bridge the gap between the garden and the kitchen below," says Fisher. At the base of the new staircase is a reclaimed iron drain.

Classic Cottage Garden

The "room" nearest the house is an English cottage garden with classic elements: flower beds, a latticework trellis, and a pair of ancient stone cannons flanking a York stone path. "I always think a garden looks better full," says Fisher. Trees—including holly, yew, and bay—delineate the cottage garden's boundaries and add vertical interest to distract the eye from the narrow width.

An Inexact Science

In the cottage garden, antique terra-
cotta edging tiles outline the beds,
planted with an artful jumble of what
Fisher calls "country-house-cliché"
flowers and shrubs. To name a few:
hydrangeas, peonies, verbena,
alliums, echinacea, and fragrant
Gertrude Jekyll roses (trained to
grow against the lattice). They all
grow together in a pleasing tangle
where the main organizing principle
is, as Fisher says, "tallest stand in
the back, please. Planting was, how
shall we say, not an exact science."

01 Windflowers

The graceful cupped flowers of Japanese anemones appear to hover in the air above long, delicate stems and add punctuation marks of color in a late-summer border. Like other varieties, 'Honorine Jobert' (with white flowers) and 'Bressingham Glow' (pink) prefer shade but will tolerate a sunny spot if it's well-drained.

02 Globe Thistles

Echinops bannaticus 'Taplow Blue' is a useful border flower because it takes up little space in a garden bed and delivers a bright punch of color with lollipop-round blue blooms. It will self-seed freely (unless deadheaded); for a more disciplined design, divide clumps in autumn.

01

02

03

03 Walled Garden

The middle garden "room" (which has a patch of green lawn and is the site of a table and chairs where Fisher and Freemantle often drink coffee) acts as a foyer to the pond beyond. Fisher said he created the walled garden after Freemantle—who had just given birth to their first child, Eliza—explained to him that in digging the pond, he hadn't fully grasped what it meant to have children. "The wall and gate followed my epiphany that water and crawling babies don't mix."

04 Exotic Import

The rectangular pond is 18 feet long but only 9 feet wide, leaving space on either side for plantings. Clumps of Australian tree ferns—popular in London, where they thrive in the mild climate—have hairy trunks and parasol fronds; their primitive wildness looks particularly exciting in the middle of a city. "We all need a touch of the exotic," says Fisher.

05 A Fine Folly

The 6-foot-6-inch-deep neoclassical pond was dug by hand; its formality is undercut by strategically placed planters perched on its ledge of York stone. "The pond was a folly, an obsession, and a complete waste of time and money. I love it," says Fisher.

04

Steal This Look
A PATINA OF AGE

01
The Real Thing

The word *fountain* is from the Latin "fons," and this one came directly from Italy to Fisher and Freemantle's garden. Procured in a swap with Fisher's friend Alessandro Stefanini, an antiques dealer, the massive stone ornament required special handling—and some ingenuity. The fountain was so heavy it fell through the floor of the truck Fisher sent to collect it. Sawed into sections for safe transport and reassembled on-site in the garden, the fountain now stands sentinel, serenely, over the koi.

02
Water Therapy

The pond is home to ornamental koi; the domesticated carp benefit from "a rather complicated" filtration system and from England's mild winters (they prefer water temperatures that do not drop below 50 degrees Fahrenheit). "The children are besotted with the fish, especially the Duke, our forty-pound koi, and love nothing more than feeding him by hand," says Fisher. "The fish take a bit of looking after, but every moment is a pleasure, and watching them is extraordinary therapy."

03
Always in Fashion

Ironwork gates, railings, and latches are all painted in Farrow & Ball's Railings, a color that makes surrounding greenery look particularly vivid.

04
Bearing Fruit

A pleached pear tree has been trained in a centuries-old manner to grow flat against a mossy redbrick garden wall.

05
Grecian Urn

Resting on a square plinth, an elegant nineteenth-century marble footed urn has a flared and molded rim above a gadrooned body. While the shape would have been familiar in a Hellenic home as that of a drinking cup for wine, here it is equally suited to a garden planter.

BROOKLYN, NEW YORK

Timeless and Treasured

A high-low mix of luxury and restraint lends a European air to Kristin Meidell's special—and very personal—Brooklyn town house garden, a gift she bequeathed to her family.

OPPOSITE: Meidell and her husband, Philip Birch, both collectors, paired a vintage beer hall dining table with classic folding metal bistro chairs from Fermob (shown here in white and available in twenty-three other colors).

Kristin Meidell was too busy living to die. After learning in 2009 that the cancer she'd faced down two years earlier was spreading, she (1) started a new job (as senior fabric designer for fashion house Reed Krakoff); (2) decided it was time for her family to buy and renovate a house in Brooklyn's Lefferts Gardens neighborhood; and (3) asked her architects for a huge picture window to overlook a tiny jewel box of a back garden. Then? She set out to create such a garden. Says her husband, Philip Birch, "Everything she did was all about living, but I knew she was doing the garden to leave for us."

Meidell knew an important design principle: pared-down plantings and a few luxurious hardscape details can make an average city backyard appear much bigger than it is. "She spent hours and hours researching," says Birch, co-owner of vintage home-furnishings store Wyeth in Manhattan. "She grew up in Southern California, and having a garden again was her passion." Meidell made a list of everything she wanted: privacy, pale-pink flowers, a barbecue grill, and pots where she and her then ten-year-old son, Emmett, could grow herbs. Then she hired a contractor to build a fence. But it didn't look quite right, so she asked Brooklyn-based garden designer Brook Klausing for advice.

"I knew right away she needed help because the contractor had chosen a boring fence—and nothing about her was boring," says Klausing. He designed a replacement with an elegant taper, which creates an optical illusion that makes the space appear larger. "She knew where she wanted to go with the garden. I just helped her get there," says Klausing. Together they made unusual high-low choices, such as paving the deck with imported black marble while forgoing a fancy grill in favor of an old-fashioned Weber. To give the garden a restrained, European air, they agreed on a row of lollipop hornbeams against the fence.

As the work progressed, however, Meidell was fading. In early spring of 2014, soon after the marble was laid, she took a photo through the picture window and posted it on Instagram with a caption: "Looking awesome." She died a few weeks later, at age forty-eight. The memorial service was in the garden.

Modern Classics

Swiss designer Willy Guhl's iconic 1954 Loop Chair is still in production; Meidell and Birch decided to buy new instead of vintage after learning that the originals were made with asbestos fibers. (Nowadays, the cement chairs are made with powdered limestone, cellulose, and synthetic fibers instead.) A single ribbon of cement, the chairs are impervious to weather and surprisingly lightweight. "It's a chair I've loved for years, and I would have put it in the living room," says Birch. "But of course she put it in its proper place, in the yard."

No Compromises

Klausing started the design process with a list: "These were her absolutes: she wanted light pink—not hot pink but *light, pale* pink—and hellebores and boxwood." With that in mind, he designed a garden with four distinct areas: twin planting beds against the house's foundation and the back fence to bookend the garden, a marble terrace, and a raised dining deck. Against that backdrop, he added details: boxwood balls ("She loved egg shapes and circles," says her husband), pale-pink hellebores growing along the fence, and a pink-blooming kousa dogwood.

01 A New Perspective

The first hardscape element that Klausing designed was a fence to define the backyard's boundaries. "We took down the other fence that didn't work, recycled the material, and designed the right thing for the space," said Klausing. The fence line tapers downward from the house toward the back of the lot, where the fence height is slightly lower than on the sides. "It's subtle," says Klausing. "The top boards get thinner and eventually disappear." He specified boards that are thinner (1 inch thick by 3½ inches wide) than typical 1-by-6-inch fence boards.

02 Dog Friendly

A planting bed of boxwood (*Buxus* 'Green Gem') and mondo grass was designed to be hardy enough to stand up to the family dog, who likes to play (and roll) in the spiky tufts. 'Green Gem' is a particularly good variety for a low hedge or to hide a foundation; it grows to a height and width of up to 3 feet and can be shaped easily if pruned two or three times a year. Low-growing mondo grass grows in clumps, making it an excellent groundcover, and its spiky leaves provide textural contrast to the boxwood balls.

01

02

Stairs Worth a Stare
Architects Kit and Philipp von Dalwig of Brooklyn-based Manifold Architecture Studio oversaw renovation of the house's interiors and also designed the graceful steel staircase with steps folded like origami. The metal staircase adds a contrasting texture to complement the brick facade and the cedar fence.

Portrait of the Artist as a Garden

After the garden was finished late in 2013, Meidell loved everything about this view from her dining room window—until one spring day when the dogwood tree bloomed. "It was hot pink instead of the barely pink she wanted, and she made Brook replace it right away," says Birch. "He brought a light pink one, and somehow he managed to find one that was still in bloom." The marble pavers inject a surprising note of glamour. Says Klausing, "We were originally going to use limestone, which is more typical for a garden, and then we found the marble. We waited a year to get it from a vendor in Turkey."

03 Eco-Friendly Hardscape

Klausing specified that both the marble
terrace and the wooden dining deck
be permeable surfaces. The marble
pavers are set on gravel ("I don't see
the point in mortaring out a patio to
force water runoff to funnel to one
drain," he says), and for the deck he
specified modular, porous panels of
ipe, an extremely dense and durable
wood that is weather- and rot-resistant.

04 Ivy League

Deciduous perennial vine Boston
ivy (*Parthenocissus tricuspidata*) is
actually a member of the grape family
and more closely related to Virginia
creeper than to evergreen ivies. Far
less invasive than its cousin Virginia
creeper, Boston ivy can reach a
height of nearly 100 feet, and its
leaves turn crimson in autumn before
dropping. The velvety foliage of a
well-established plant can protect a
facade from the heat of the sun and cut
air-conditioning costs in summer.

Designer at Work

Klausing, watering the rosemary shrubs planted at the base of the pale-pink dogwood tree, says, "Normally I like a garden that's looser and wilder, but this one called for editing and a minimalist style that still somehow is super cozy." The juxtaposition of sharp square corners and soft round shapes (such as the grill and the pots of herbs that mother and son planted together) pleases the eye.

Timeless and Treasured

Thirteen Gardens We Love

Steal This Look
INSTANT CLASSICS

01
Waterfront Style

A vintage caged wharf light was made by the Russell & Stoll Co., industrial lighting and marine fixture manufacturers that also made wall-mounted fixtures for New York City's subway stations in the first decades of the twentieth century. Known for sturdy, well-made designs, the company was founded by Brooklyn residents F. J. Russell and Theodore Stoll in 1902.

02
Meals on Wheels

Klausing's original plan called for a built-in outdoor kitchen for Meidell, who grew up in Southern California. "It was going to take a long time to get that piece of furniture, so I got a Weber grill and surprised her with it," says Birch. Meidell decided not to replace the Weber after all because, she said, it was portable and didn't take up much space.

03
Still Life with Staghorn

An edible fig tree in a pot has clumps of *Carex pensylvanica* planted, like a shaggy rug, to cover its roots. Along with the mounted staghorn ferns on the fence, the fig needs to come indoors during cold winter months. In the narrow bed at the base of the fence are perennial hellebores; you have to look under their leaves to see the pale-pink flowers.

04
Jingle Bells

New York City–based ceramicist Michele Quan makes decorative wheel-thrown jingle bells that hang on lengths of hemp rope. Available in a variety of colors and paint finishes, her hollow bells produce a resonant ring (hence their name) when touched and may be hung singly or in clusters in the garden.

05
For the Birds

Lucky birds. Inspired by the clean minimalist lines of one of the twentieth century's most iconic buildings, Danish designer Monique Engelund created a bird feeder that evokes the pavilion that Ludwig Mies van der Rohe designed for the Barcelona Exposition in 1929. A modern classic in its own right, Engelund's Barcelona bird feeder on a pole is made of weather-resistant acacia wood and aluminum.

A Low-Maintenance Weekend Retreat

Inspired by a nearby land preserve that covers nearly a third of Shelter Island, Suzanne Shaker and Pete Dandridge designed a simple garden with outdoor spaces to dine, lounge, and grow plants—all without disturbing the natural surroundings.

OPPOSITE: During the week, Shaker and Dandridge live and work a hundred miles east in New York City. "I say to people who complain that it's horrible to get here that, yes, it's terrible," Shaker admits. "And to the people I invite to visit, I say, 'You get on a ferry and leave it all behind, and it's so wonderful.'"

When Suzanne Shaker and Pete Dandridge bought an acre of land on which to build a house on Shelter Island, off the eastern tip of Long Island, the property was densely covered with trees, wetlands, and native shrubs. Dandridge, an art conservator at the Metropolitan Museum of Art in New York City, appreciated the quality of the light. And Shaker, an interior designer, trusted his instincts. "To me, it looked like a lot of muddy land and brown trees," she admits. But as they planned and built a small, modern house on the site, she came to understand—and love— all aspects of the surrounding landscape. Consider the "backyard," for example. At the base of a slope is a swampy patch that Shaker was originally inclined to describe as a mud hole. "Then one day an artist friend came over and said, 'You have a vernal pond,' and I thought, 'My God, what a beautiful expression,' and the mud hole took on a whole new meaning."

"Less is more" is the mantra that informed all the choices for the weekend house's garden, designed to blend in rather than compete with the surrounding landscape and nearby two-thousand-acre nature preserve. Dandridge planned and built most of the hardscape—including a front patio, paths, and a large garden bed where herbs and cutting flowers consort freely—which by definition meant that changes came at a measured pace. "Pete is very methodical, and he marked out the shape of the patio with stakes and sight lines before he started," says Shaker. "Every time we were at the house, I would hear this *tap, tap, tap* from the tool he used to pound in the pavers. Then one day, suddenly, it was done." The result is an unobtrusive garden that takes advantage of available space, light, and local materials. It suits not only the house and the preservationist ethos of Shelter Island but also its owners, who come out from the city year-round, in all kinds of weather, to spend time with their vernal pond.

Ultimate High-Low House

When it was time to build a house, New York City–based architect Deborah Berke took on Shaker's self-described "much-too-small" job because they are friends. Berke (who has since become dean of the Yale School of Architecture) designed a 1,240-square-foot box of wood and glass—a dramatic visual contrast to the surrounding woodlands. Stylish budget-friendly choices include a galvanized metal roof, brushed aluminum windows, a raised deck that serves as a front stoop (the planks are Trex, a composite material that "lasts forever" and means "you never get splinters," says Shaker), and a patio large enough to afford space both to dine and to lounge around in chaises.

Sounds of Summer

The front entrance leads to a glass breezeway that divides the house into two separate wings: living quarters and a master bedroom suite. Full-height glass doors allow visitors to see all the way through the house and into the backyard. Installing the pair of wooden screen doors was a challenge, but the couple wanted to avoid metal. ("We wanted the feeling of summer, and that meant wood," says Shaker.) To fit the doorway opening, Dandridge designed and built a simple pair of cedar screen doors that swing out and slam shut with the aid of four commercial-grade aluminum and metal springs from the hardware store.

01 Deer-Defeating Garden

Dandridge designed and built the large garden bed that runs the length of the front patio. The bed borders the seating area with a mix of strongly scented, deer-deterring plants, including herbs—such as sage, chives, and rosemary—and ornamental cutting flowers such as alliums (members of the onion family). "We have tons of deer but have not had to put up fencing," says Shaker.

02 Blue Perfume

A late-summer bloomer, vividly blue *Caryopteris* 'Dark Knight' adds color and fragrance to a garden bed in August and early September, and its nectar proves irresistible to butterflies and bees.

03 Multipurpose Furniture

Teak dining furniture stays outdoors year-round, weathering to a soft silver gray to complement the facade of the house. Chaises from Donghia (a model no longer in production) flatten to become long benches when more seating is required. For a similar style, San Francisco–based furniture designer Henry Hall's Pure Chaise has an adjustable back that transforms from chair to bench.

A Low-Maintenance Weekend Retreat

Thirteen Gardens We Love

04

04 Green Acres

Behind the house is a shaded viewing platform—with butterfly chairs from Circa50 and a Pawley's Island hammock—overlooking the vernal pond.

05 Night Lights

BEGA, a family-owned German company, has been manufacturing high-quality lights since 1945. Shaker and Dandridge installed the company's pathway luminaires, made of die-cast aluminum with a black matte finish. The unobtrusive fixtures direct beams of pure white LED light downward to avoid a searchlight effect.

05

Gentle Giants

After building the house, Shaker and Dandridge planted 7-foot-tall specimens of fast-growing *Cedrus deodara* trees to screen the property's perimeter. Fourteen years later, the evergreen Himalayan natives are 30 feet high (and at maturity could reach 60 feet). With their pyramidal shapes and gently drooping branches, the trees create a soft, blue-green backdrop for the silver-stained house.

Steal This Look
QUIET DETAILS

01
Low-Maintenance Planter

Impervious to rain and snow, a shallow concrete planter stays outdoors year-round. It is filled with moss and succulents, including hens and chicks, which often survive the winter "if the squirrels don't bury their nuts in them," says Shaker.

02
Informal Elegance

Shaker serves homemade lemonade flavored with a stem of lemon verbena from her garden. Mismatched glassware adds to the casual charm of afternoon drinks served outdoors.

03
Hose Corral

To keep the garden hose neatly wound, Shaker bought a clay pot at Marders nursery in Bridgehampton. The vessel is big enough to hide the hose, but with its natural color and low-slung look, it's unobtrusive in its spot next to the front walkway. Dandridge drilled a hole in the pot and threaded the hose through to attach it to the water spigot.

04
Squirreled Away

To save the birds' supper from squirrels, Dandridge ran a thin wire from a tree branch, hung a hardware-store hook at the end, and suspended a rustproof metal tube bird feeder from the hook. From a distance, it looks like a magic trick: "You can't figure out how it is hanging there," says Shaker.

05
Life as Art

Unearthed on the property during construction, a boulder-size souvenir rock found a permanent home at the edge of the patio, where its Noguchi-esque silhouette invokes contemplation of the peaceful surrounding woodlands.

Posh and Pampered Indoor Greenhouse

Famous for her glamorously minimalist interiors, London designer Rose Uniacke rescued an unloved indoor gallery in her nineteenth-century mansion, creating a light-filled conservatory that evokes an era when Victorian plant hunters roamed the globe in search of the exotic.

OPPOSITE: As you enter the house, Uniacke's glass-roofed conservatory is the first room you see, visible through four pairs of arched glass doors. (Although the doors look steel-framed, they actually are finely constructed in wood by English artisans.) The house's original owner, Scottish high-society portrait painter James Rannie Swinton (1816–1888), would usher clients into the high-ceilinged room to view his work. If they were suitably impressed and commissioned a painting, they would sit for a portrait in his adjoining studio.

The Georgian Revival–style villa that London interior designer and antiques dealer Rose Uniacke and her husband, film producer David Heyman, bought in 2007 had fallen on unfortunate times. Divided into apartments, it had an ugly staircase, fire-door partitions—and an odd domed gallery in the center of the main floor. But Uniacke (who trained as a furniture restorer, gilder, and specialist in paint and lacquer finishes before opening her eponymous shop on London's premiere antiques row on Pimlico Road) was up for the challenge. Known for the serenely restrained interiors she creates for clients including Victoria and David Beckham and perfumier Jo Malone, Uniacke hired Belgian minimalist architect Vincent Van Duysen to reimagine the space.

And thus was born the luxuriously rustic conservatory that Uniacke calls the Winter Garden. The first step in transforming the gallery was to remove an inferior 1970s glass roof from the classical domed ceiling. "Suddenly the ceiling seemed vastly higher," says Uniacke. "It radically changed the feel of the space. The proportions of the room became fabulous."

Discovering that the original wooden rafters were still in place, she had them wire-brushed clean and left them exposed. Layers of plaster were stripped from the walls, revealing beautiful bare brick that Uniacke left raw. She furnished the space with a mix of antiques from her shop.

To choose plants for the indoor garden, Uniacke brought in Tom Stuart-Smith, London's landscape designer of the moment. Stuart-Smith (who also designed an outdoor garden space on a walled terrace along one side of the house) was "in charge of shape and planting and the mechanics," says Uniacke.

Stuart-Smith wanted to make the space as relaxed and informal as possible, given its grand scale. "All the planting was scattered around with apparent abandon in a variety of containers," he says. A mix of orchids, tropical plants, and climbing vines creates a room that Uniacke calls "totally unexpected."

The Heart of the Matter

The garden conservatory is where Uniacke and her family entertain, eat together, read, and arrange flowers. The glass in the doors was specially made to copy the wavy, imperfect panes found in old Georgian houses. "It's essential to make all the details interesting," says Uniacke.

01 Flooded with Light

Uniacke worked with Van Duysen to design a skylight that looks as if it could have been lifted from a Victorian greenhouse. The only window in the room, it was designed to be a visual focal point and has overlapping wavy glass tiles (laid the same way as slate tiles on a roof). Even the exposed heating pipes at the base of the skylight are beautiful; they're copper and glow in sunlight.

02 A Repurposed Fountain

Uniacke's favorite planter was originally a fountain, most likely made in England. Set on a massive stone base, it's copper with a patina of verdigris, the greenish tinge that appears when some metals are exposed to the air as they age. A pure example of Japonism, it hails from the late nineteenth century, when English taste was powerfully influenced by Japanese arts and crafts.

03 Brick and Metal

Most of the furnishings in the Winter Garden—the table, chairs, light fixtures, and candelabra—are made of forged and beaten metal, a material that lends an outdoor air to an indoor room. Exposed brick walls have a similar effect. The climbing plant on the wall to the right is *Cissus rhombifolia*, or oak-leaf ivy, which thrives in low light.

01

02

03

Dining Out, Indoors

A vintage French steel conservatory table is the site of frequent family meals. Uniacke calls the table, with its patina of green paint, a "wonderful workhorse." Patinated bronze chairs, designed by a Swiss sculptor and furniture designer, date from the 1950s. A dwarf palm (*Phoenix roebelenii*) lends a tropical air, as does the small-leafed *Ficus pumila* (creeping fig) climbing the wall between the doors.

Posh and Pampered Indoor Greenhouse

Thirteen Gardens We Love

04

05

04 The Statement Plant

One of Stuart-Smith's signature design techniques is to focus attention on a single dramatic plant, in this case a *Ficus lyrata*, or fiddle-leaf fig, with bold foliage.

05 Hothouse Flowers

Uniacke, who chooses all the room's orchids, likes a mix of varieties (almost always green and white). Shown here is a phalaenopsis (also known as a moth orchid); its long-lasting blooms can persevere for up to four months. All orchids require excellent drainage and adequate humidity (Stuart-Smith had a misting system installed in the roof after realizing that the air in the conservatory was too dry).

Secret Garden

Uniacke also has an outdoor garden, a walled terrace along one side of the house. Because it was very low and disconnected from the house, Stuart-Smith lifted the level by 3 feet. He paved the floor with old York stone (sandstone quarried in Yorkshire) and flanked the doorway with two euphorbia shrubs. *Euphorbia x pasteurii* is a "new-ish variety," with yellow, honey-scented flowers in late spring.

07

06 A Layered Look

A mix of different planters and types of foliage gives this space an informal air. A mature olive tree thrives in a deep terra-cotta pot. Against the brick wall, Stuart-Smith planted camellias, southern magnolia, and evergreen *Eriobotrya* shrubs to create solid texture and enclose the space with greenery.

07 Ingredients at Hand

When Uniacke bought the property, it already had an ivy-covered facade, where vines of wisteria and Virginia creeper intertwined. The carved stone pedestal urn is another vintage find, and many of the smaller pots hold herbs that Uniacke uses when she cooks.

Steal This Look

RUSTIC GLAMOUR

01

Hidden Door

Uniacke loved the exposed brick walls and didn't want the look spoiled by a door. But there *was* a door; how else would one get into the octagonal room beyond (the original owner's painting studio)? To make the door disappear, Uniacke hired movie-set builders to create a trompe l'oeil version. They took an imprint from a section of wall, converted it into fiberglass, and attached it to the existing door.

02

A Touch of Venice

The two hanging lanterns are Venetian and date from the late nineteenth century. (Two similar lanterns hang in the hallway just outside the conservatory.) Uniacke had them wired for electricity.

03
Antique Sphinxes

This cast-iron planter was made in the late nineteenth century by Paris's renowned Antoine Durenne Foundry. Uniacke sourced the provenance: "We have the original drawings, and we believe these are copies taken from the originals at Versailles." Winged sphinxes form handles—but lifting this solid metal piece is no mean feat. The delicate fronds of a maidenhair fern are a visual counterbalance to the planter's heft.

04
Power Seating

The backless design of these cast-iron curule chairs originated in ancient Rome, where the chair was considered the "magistrate's seat," or seat of power. (Napoléon also was partial to the style.) Uniacke's chairs are French, with mesh seats and a green painted finish improved by age.

05
Flattering Candlelight

A bronze candelabra, one of a pair, is modeled after ancient Roman versions found at Pompeii. Uniacke thinks hers were cast by the legendary Chiurazzi Foundry in Naples, which was launched in 1870 and still specializes in fine reproductions of classic works. She does know that the pair were made for Yvette Guilbert (1865–1944), a French cabaret singer who headlined at the Moulin Rouge and was a favored subject of Toulouse-Lautrec's.

A Painterly Landscape

For their thirty-five-acre weekend retreat in upstate New York, landscape designer Lucien Rees Roberts and architect Steven Harris pored over topographical maps to create a park-like landscape that celebrates the land's best features and evokes the English countryside of Rees Roberts's childhood.

OPPOSITE: Rees Roberts collaborated with landscape designer Margie Ruddick to lay out the gravel driveway. The two also reconfigured the hill a little. (Why not? Harris had rented a bulldozer and driver as a birthday gift for Rees Roberts.) The first part of the house was completed in 1991, with a second structure (with a matching 14-by-40-foot footprint) added in 2005. The buildings' modest size creates an interesting trick of scale, making the landscape look bigger. Lead-coated copper roofs were chosen for their soft gray color and matte finish. An underground passage links the two buildings.

More than twenty-five years ago, Lucien Rees Roberts and his partner (now husband), Steven Harris, decided to build themselves a country retreat. In their search for the perfect piece of land, they had a number of criteria. It needed to be a pleasant drive from their home base in New York City ("There goes Long Island," jokes Harris), and it had to be at a high elevation with long rolling views to suit Rees Roberts's painterly sensibility. He grew up in the same part of England that was home to both architect Edwin Lutyens and garden designer Gertrude Jekyll and "was used to going on long walks in the countryside, where you'd always have the right-of-way on other people's property," he says.

After combing through U.S. Geological Survey maps, Rees Roberts found the land—thirty-five acres of field and woods on a hill outside Kinderhook, in New York's Columbia County. The gentle hills and valleys invited rambling and offered panoramic views of the Catskills and the Berkshires. With the help of New York–based landscape designer Margie Ruddick, Rees Roberts regraded parts of the land. Meanwhile, Harris (whose company is Steven Harris Architects) designed a shingled house that looks like a modern version of the old barns that dot the surrounding countryside.

The house sits on the property's highest point. Surrounding it is Rees Roberts's garden, which is essentially "managed wilderness," in the words of landscape designer David Kelly, who works at Rees Roberts + Partners. Even a patio next to the house is carpeted in untamed drifts of creeping thyme. With Kelly's help, Rees Roberts planted a meadow of wildflowers through which paths into the woods are mown. (For more about the meadow, see "Sunny Notes in a Wildflower Meadow Garden" on page 197.) The overall effect is one of an effortless, undulating landscape. Here, says Rees Roberts, "there are endless variations of how you can walk the land," circling the entire perimeter without realizing it because there are no fences or boundary markers.

Magic Carpet
The largest "room" in the house? The terrace, covered in permeable concrete pavers, planted with perennial creeping thyme, and punctuated by a Cortland apple tree from Windy Hill Farm, a nursery in the Berkshires. The pale-gray color of the window frames is Benjamin Moore's Winterwood; the shingles are covered in an opaque white stain made by Olympic.

01 Far and Wide

The kitchen window looks onto a swath of grass and a wall of Catskill fieldstone. The Vermont Imperial Danby marble on the kitchen counter is prized for its soft gray and gold veins. The exterior overhang was planned as a design element but also affords shade, as the window faces south.

02 Sleight of Hand

Built to look dry-stacked, a retaining wall is wider at the bottom for stability, and has concealed mortar joints.

A Breezeway for Dining

The dining room welcomes hillside breezes when the barn doors and 14-foot-wide glass doors are open on both sides. (There are also screens to keep out insects, if necessary.) The doorstep is Imperial Danby marble from Vermont Quarries, which has been used for houses in the Northeast for more than a century.

Lawn Games

The mown lawn may look innocuous, but it's the site of cutthroat weekend croquet matches. The croquet set is from Jaques of London, a company that claims to have invented the game, introducing it to the world in 1851. It was a sixtieth-birthday gift for Harris, who despite his American heritage loves croquet almost as much as Rees Roberts, calling it "a blood sport for the British."

A Mysterious Shore

"There are a lot of ponds up here," says Harris, "and I hate most of them because you can see the entire perimeter. Look at the ponds in New York's Central Park: they're not big, but you can never see the whole thing from one vantage point." Kelly designed this two-acre manmade pond to look natural, using boulders unearthed during the house excavation to make a rocky beach and a spot where you can dive into a 25-foot-deep pool.

03

03 Sunset Strip

The fire pit is the place to gather for drinks while the sun is setting, with stunning views of the Catskills and the Berkshires. The gently curving back of the concrete bench is a wall of local fieldstone.

04 Ring of Fire

Kelly lined the fire pit with Catskill fieldstone and planted *Rhus aromatica*, or fragrant sumac, a deciduous shrub that attracts birds and butterflies—but not deer, an important factor on this unfenced estate.

04

Steal This Look
THYME TERRACE

01
Midcentury Modern Seating

A wire-mesh Sculptura side chair by Russell Woodard dates from the 1960s. "They're not making these anymore," says Rees Roberts, "so we snap them up whenever we see them for sale. We probably have eight by now." Because they are left outdoors, the chairs need to be repainted every few years. (The Biscayne outdoor armchair by Philadelphia-based Lostine is uncannily similar.)

02
Glamorous Cinder Blocks

Concrete paving blocks called Grasscrete, originally designed for parking lots, have openings in the blocks. Planted with grass or other ground cover, the blocks make an environmentally friendly surface.

03
Water Saver

The original plan was to grow grass on the Grasscrete terrace, so a Rain Bird irrigation system was installed. Then came the inspired idea to plant creeping thyme instead. Due to its Mediterranean origins, the herb doesn't need much water, and it loves the full sun it gets on the terrace. (It also thrives in what Kelly calls "the crappy soil.")

04
Better Than Grass

A low-maintenance perennial ground cover, creeping thyme blooms from midspring through early summer and scents the air all summer. Though visitors are sometimes reluctant to walk on it, the herb doesn't take offense—in fact, it rewards every step by releasing more fragrance.

05
Bring on the Butterflies

A patch of 'Hidcote' lavender grows on the terrace in a gap deliberately left to accommodate it. This variety is "right on the cusp" for the region's climate, says Kelly—some years it winters over; sometimes it doesn't survive and has to be replanted in spring. The strong scent attracts butterflies.

A Fairy-Tale Garden in the City

In the backyard of Michelle McKenna and Brenlen Jinkens's restored 1840s London town house is an enchanting garden where butterflies, bees, and beneficials feel at home thanks to a mossy roof garden, flowering trees, and the occasional china teacup turned bird feeder.

OPPOSITE: Surrounding the property are five-hundred-year-old plane trees that cast quite a bit of shade onto McKenna and Jinkens's garden. To make a back corner sunnier, McKenna cut down an ailing willow tree (but kept the stump to use as a stool).

A remodel left Michelle McKenna and Brenlen Jinkens's bulldozer-scarred garden looking "just like a war zone," remembers McKenna. Having grown up in Ireland, where landscapes look like bolts of green velvet, she wanted to transform her backyard in London's Clerkenwell neighborhood into a whimsical and very verdant garden "to honor the nature spirits," she says. But with the heavy equipment and construction debris cleared away, all that was left were a few ailing trees and a cinder-block wall around the perimeter of the corner lot.

First order of business: the garden needed a backdrop for greenery. Should the couple replace the cinder-block wall? they wondered. Or could they get by with plantings to hide its surface? "We agonized, because a new wall of old London brick is quite expensive. But in the end, we replaced the wall, and it was one of our better decisions," McKenna says. Next, their contractor built a terrace and wide wooden steps to connect the garden to their first-floor parlor, and removed a derelict shed in favor of a tiny cottage (where McKenna, a practitioner of the Japanese healing art *amatsu*, could see clients).

Then McKenna designed a garden to delight her three children, with magical touches that include a cluster of tiny bee houses, a miniature raspberry bramble to explore, and ripe fruit hanging at eye level. McKenna's friend Margaret Willis, a horticulturalist who also owns a nearby antiques shop, Vintage Heaven & Cakehole, helped pick the plants. "She's been a practicing Buddhist for years and years, and that also brought another kind of spiritual energy to the garden," says McKenna. The result is a happy tangle of heirloom roses, butterfly bushes, and cottage garden flowers that spill onto the pathways.

Eschewing straight lines and sharp corners for gentler curves and waves, McKenna and Jinkens laid out a branching path to lure visitors into nooks and crannies, where they are sure to find the unexpected: a fragrant climbing rose, a garden gnome hiding among the flowers, or a teacup bird feeder with painted china cups. "The surprises are quite sweet, especially when you come upon cherries to pick," says McKenna.

Into That Lovely Garden
Carpeted with mossy turf grass, the garden evokes McKenna's Irish roots. Rambling paths (paved with recycled slate chips) lead visitors on a tour of the perimeter and also cut across the lawn to destinations such as an outbuilding McKenna uses as a treatment room. "I trained in Japanese osteopathy, a practice that is part of a martial arts tradition, used to help ninjas when they come in with injuries," she says.

01　Reclaimed Wood

During construction, the builders unearthed a portion of an old tree trunk, which McKenna repurposed as a support beam for the outbuilding that replaced an old shed. To get the two panes of glass to meet seamlessly at the edge of the trunk was "quite a tricky job," she says, but worth it for the uninterrupted views.

02　Powdery Pinks

Button-shaped pink scabiosa flowers tangle with grasses in a flowerbed. In a mild climate like London's, scabiosa is a perennial flower you can count on for several summers of repeat blooms.

Strings of Light

A string of Japanese lanterns (purchased on Etsy) are powered by rooftop solar panels, tilted in a southerly direction to capture maximum sunlight. The outbuilding's facade is sided with strips of oak and has a round window whose shape echoes other curves in the landscape. "There is really no straight line anywhere in the garden," says McKenna.

03

03 Woodcutter's Bench

"We struggled for a while searching for garden furniture because we wanted something quite organic in shape," says McKenna. The one-of-a-kind bench made from reclaimed wood came from Free Range Designs in Wales, a company known for making whimsical furniture, including a storytelling chair for chef Jamie Oliver and garden furniture for Nelson Mandela.

04 Pansy Pots

At the base of the bench is a group of cheerfully lawless plants in mismatched pots, including variegated ivy, heathers, and pansies.

04

Bees Welcome

A collection of bee houses hangs above a second raised planting bed, which serves as the family's edible garden, filled with a bramble of raspberry canes, rhubarb, strawberry plants, and herbs.

Steal This Look

WHIMSICAL TOUCHES

01
Outdoor Art Club

A pair of 15-by-15-inch plaster tiles with flower friezes are by London-based artist and theater prop maker Rachel Dein of Tactile Studio. To make the one-of-a-kind tiles, Dein lays flowers such as alliums (shown) on a slab of clay and presses them to create a mold. After removing the flowers, Dein pours plaster into the mold to create a relief. She sells similar tiles on Etsy.

02
Special Treats

Tucked here and there in the garden beds, McKenna places terra-cotta pots (this one planted with variegated ivy) and half-hidden garden ornaments and statuary.

03
No Vacancy

McKenna collects bee houses of various sizes and designs, many of which she purchases from Rowen & Wren. In the larger houses, rows of hollow bamboo strips attract mason bees, who nest in the open tubes.

04
Mad Hatter's Luncheon

Mounted on the brick wall, chipped china cups from Vintage Heaven & Cakehole hold birdseed ("although it's the squirrels that usually help themselves," says McKenna) and hang from the branches of one of the old trees cut down to make way for the garden.

05
Benevolent Spirits

Throughout the garden, McKenna hangs outdoor art on the brick walls. A plaster pair hung by the gate depicts the Green Man of folklore (a keeper of nature spirits) and Mother Nature and greets visitors as they enter the garden.

Old Hollywood, New Glamour

With the help of LA landscape designer Matthew Brown, Commune Design principals (and siblings) Ramin and Pam Shamshiri deftly modernized a 1920s Hollywood garden while preserving a veneer of nostalgia and mystery.

OPPOSITE: Inspired by the ornate tile mosaics they saw while visiting the Alhambra in Granada, Spain, Pam and Ramin Shamshiri designed a Moorish-style courtyard fountain with mosaic tile from Ann Sacks.

Morocco meets Old Hollywood sounds more like a flea-market mash-up than the guiding design principle behind one of California's most glamorous modern gardens—until you step through the gate of the Los Angeles home of Donna Langley and Ramin Shamshiri.

The story of this charming and unlikely garden began nearly a decade ago, when Shamshiri (one of four cofounders of Commune Design, the firm whose relaxed eclecticism has transformed the face of California design) fell hard for a 1920s Spanish Colonial–style stucco house that had been homogenized by an unfortunate 1980s remodel. At first nobody else saw the potential. Not his wife (the chairwoman of Universal Pictures). Not his sister (Commune Design cofounder Pam Shamshiri). And not landscape designer Matthew Brown, who pronounced the oddly shaped property with a brambly old two-tier garden "not that interesting."

But after Commune Design gave a face-lift to the interior of the 3,600-square-foot house in the Los Feliz foothills, brother and sister joined forces with Brown to renovate the old garden. And that's when things *did* get interesting.

For the Los Feliz garden, the goal was to transform rambling, unused spaces at different elevations into outdoor rooms with a purpose—"In LA, there's no excuse not to be outside year-round," says Brown. The biggest inspiration for the project was a recent visit the Shamshiri siblings had made to Spain, where the Alhambra's Moorish tiles and fountains evinced a glamour well-suited to the Mediterranean climate of Southern California.

The changes started in the front yard, where a gracious, rounded front stoop with tiled stairs now welcomes visitors. On the property's lower level is a new swimming pool, the mature California pepper trees around it judiciously pruned to create sun-splashed shade canopies. But the biggest transformation is evident in a courtyard garden accessible from several rooms in the house. There, new walls—almost cartoonish in their exaggerated height—provide privacy, and a patterned tile floor flows uninterrupted between inside and out to make the low-ceiling indoor rooms appear more spacious.

Optical Illusion
In the shady courtyard, a low perimeter curb outlines garden beds where ficus trees are underplanted with mother ferns, liriope, and spiky red-leafed cordyline. In the dining area, a travertine-topped table from LA-based furniture designers 10Ten is paired with vintage Sol y Luna armless chairs designed in 1954 by Dan Johnson as part of his Gazelle collection (a cast-aluminum version is currently manufactured by Brown Jordan).

Hanging Gardens

The most dramatic addition to the garden? By extending the height of the courtyard walls by 7 feet, the designers created a private area for outdoor cooking, dining, and living where the family spends much of the day. Vines including needlepoint ivy and creeping fig cascade from planter troughs on top of the walls (where a drip irrigation system keeps everything watered). California clay sculptor Stan Bitters designed a tall, narrow fireplace with a tiled wall mural, which develops a glossy ebony patina from smoke (and is easily washed off).

A Shady Spot

Influenced by childhood memories of the outdoor Persian tearooms in Tehran, Pam Shamshiri created a relaxed side porch with mismatched furniture that obeys a simple rule: keep seating heights the same so everyone is at eye level. Artist Stan Bitters's clay wind chimes act as a screen and reinforce the shady coolness, and two large juniper bonsais flank the seating area.

01

01 Sun Worshippers

To take advantage of the fact that the pool receives full sun most of the day, Brown planted succulents in pots along its edge.

02 Waterworks

LA-based architect Bruce Bolander designed the swimming pool for the lower level of the property, which previously had been an overgrown, inaccessible area of the garden. Surrounding the pool are judiciously pruned mature California pepper trees (*Schinus molle*) and old-growth *Pittosporum tobira* shrubs that Brown suspects were planted in the 1920s when the house was built. An airy canopy of branches casts dappled shade on a permeable patio with black cantera stone pavers set in a herringbone pattern and "grouted" with plugs of turf grass.

Steal This Look
MOROCCAN MODERN

01
Curb Appeal

During the remodel, a solid front door was replaced by a glass panel covered with decorative scrollwork to bring sunlight into the house. Reclaimed patterned ceramic tile announces the house's East-meets-West influences. Glazed ceramic planters are from Inner Gardens nursery and garden shop in nearby Culver City; the pots' striking turquoise hue unifies the collection of varied heights and shapes.

02
Flea Market Find

A vintage find, a simple brass tap serves as a spout for the fountain.

03
Casbah Chic

Vintage stamped-metal Moroccan lanterns are enhanced by their patina of rust. For a similar metal lantern with glass panels, LA-based Badia Design sells a selection of both its classic and contemporary Moroccan designs online.

04
Eclectic Details

An enormous donkey's tail succulent (*Sedum morganianum*) grows in a giant clamshell; it thrives in full sun and requires little water. Brown frequently purchases specimen plants from Tropics Inc. nursery in Santa Monica, a go-to destination for designers searching for unusual succulents.

05
Night Magic

Metal cutwork lanterns hold tea lights and are a modern version of filigree Moroccan lanterns used elsewhere in the space; originally, these were designed to cast lacy patterns onto the ceiling and walls of tents.

Shades of Gray in the City

In Brooklyn's Prospect Heights neighborhood, creative director Mariza Scotch and fitness trainer Dièry Prudent stripped their garden of color to create a space that remains luxuriantly evergreen.

OPPOSITE: From the street, the prim demeanor of Scotch and Prudent's four-story Edith Wharton–era brownstone gives no hint of the double lot that makes their garden twice as deep as the average 20-by-40-foot city backyard. On the restored facade of the 1871 town house, glossy black window trim unites the banisters, fence, and gate.

They still have the Polaroid they snapped the first time they saw their Brooklyn brownstone nearly twenty years ago. In the fading photo, Mariza Scotch and Dièry Prudent can see the years of garden neglect—a ratty patch of grass and a tree scarred by lightning—and the secret you can't guess from the street: the double-deep lot has a nearly hundred-foot-long backyard that seems endless. "We were coming from a small apartment, and the ridiculous proportion of it made us feel like we had discovered magic in the middle of the city," says Scotch.

Harnessing the magic took some effort, though. Their first attempts failed. "We do a lot of traveling and we used to have sort of a sad annual cycle where in May or June we'd populate the garden with plants, then go away, then come home to find a death field," says Scotch.

Scotch, a former handbag designer who is chief creative director for accessories brand Skagen Denmark, started collecting photos of the sort of garden the couple wanted: a serene space where they could entertain and Prudent, a fitness trainer, could coach clients. Inspired by the minimalist design of the sculpture garden at the Noguchi Museum (one of her favorite spots in the city), Scotch wanted "shades of gray, surface texture, a certain austerity that would allow the plant materials to look very rich against the gray." When she came across a photo of a simple, modern garden by designers Susan Welti and Paige Keck, it seemed just right, prompting her to contact the two owners of Brooklyn-based Foras Studio.

Welti came over to take a look and immediately saw the possibilities of creating a dramatic focal point: "The thing I remember from the first time I laid eyes on the garden was the incredible old pine tree—really remarkable, gnarly, with odd reaching angles to it—and it was clear from that moment that everything else had to bow down to the pine tree." Nearly four years later, the gray and green garden is a backdrop that makes everything that comes into it—sunlight, people, food—look more intense. Says Scotch, "Now when we come home after a trip, it's a welcoming moment."

The Center of Attention
A blue-needled *Pinus strobus*
(eastern white pine tree), which
under ideal conditions can reach
a height of 250 feet and live
250 years. Like most old trees, this
one needed help after a lightning
strike and a subsequent ice storm.
Scotch and Prudent coaxed it back
to health by loosening compacted
earth, conditioning the soil with
minerals and organic matter, and
protecting shallow roots with a layer
of permeable crushed stone.

Silver Tones

Welti and Keck created calm by restricting the hardscape to gray materials, including weathered cedar, bluestone pavers, and gravel. Laid out on a grid, all roads lead to the pine tree. The designers also created distinct outdoor "rooms" for dining, entertaining, and fitness sessions (with Prudent's equipment hidden behind a bamboo hedge in the back). Welti took advantage of a natural bower of existing Japanese maple trees to create both shade and light (from strings of industrial-grade café lights) above the dining table.

A Sculpturing of Space

Scotch and Prudent asked for a design that would reflect the minimalist philosophy of landscape architect Isamu Noguchi, who saw gardens as "sculpturing of space: a beginning, and a groping to another level of sculptural experience and use: a total sculpture space experience beyond individual sculptures." Shrubs including *Taxus baccata* 'Repandens' near the fence and two varieties of boxwood (*Buxus* 'Justin Brouwers' and *Buxus* 'Green Velvet') function as individually molded elements as well as sculpted features of a unified landscape.

01 Reuse, Reuse, Reuse

When Scotch and Prudent bought the house, bluestone pavers were scattered throughout the garden, the remains of pathways from an earlier era. Contractor Jeremy Siegel collected them and fit the pieces together like a puzzle to create a wide walkway leading from the house to the backyard dining area. The pavers are set into the ground at a depth of 2½ inches in a base of crushed bluestone to create a permeable path edged with custom-cut steel strips.

02 The Power of Symmetry

A bed of tightly clipped symmetrical balls of *Buxus* 'Green Velvet' is evergreen, providing color year-round. A hardy variety of boxwood (more resistant to disease than English box), it is a good choice for town house gardens because it also tolerates shade well. 'Green Velvet' can grow as tall as 4 feet but is kept low here to function as an edging plant. To maintain its tight, symmetrical shape, the couple prunes it three times a year.

An Open-Air Gym

A bamboo hedge provides privacy for Prudent's outdoor fitness center, which is tucked into the back of the yard beneath the pine tree. The green hedge is a more graceful way to demarcate the space than a fence: "Bamboo can be unruly," says Welti, "and we intentionally used it to create some messiness to soften the garden." Uniformly sized bluestone pavers match the color of the main walkway.

03 Bench Press

Contractor Jeremy Siegel made the bluestone bench for Prudent's clients to use during training sessions. The base was made from two sawn slabs and the seat from a rough slab with tumbled edges. Prudent collects vintage cast-iron hand weights, kettlebells, and dumbbells from sources such as eBay and Etsy.

04 A Fitnest for Fitness

Prudent and Scotch designed a collapsible apparatus called the Fitnest, built with fence support posts and adjustable bars on which clients can do pull-ups and lunges. "It's a very simple contraption," says Scotch. "The whole thing comes apart, and the pieces can fit in a channel under the boardwalk. When it's put away, all you see are two little stone plugs in the patio, and it looks like nothing was ever there."

Shades of Gray in the City

Thirteen Gardens We Love

Steal This Look

ZEN MINIMALISM

01

A Wall of Windows

Integral to Prudent and Scotch's vision of a seamless indoor-outdoor living space is a stretch of floor-to-ceiling windows that replaced the house's back wall at garden level. The custom metal-framed windows designed by Manhattan-based Murdock Solon Architects swivel 180 degrees to allow unobstructed egress to the backyard.

02

A Minimalist Dining Table

Scotch designed the Corten steel and cedar dining table, which, she says, is "heavily influenced" by one of her favorite designers, Donald Judd. The table's support trusses are ¼-inch mild steel, which is designed to develop a rust-colored patina over time. The cedar slab top was left unfinished, like the deck, to weather naturally along with the rest of the garden materials.

03
Hedge Effect

Small hornbeam trees
(*Carpinus caroliniana*) planted
in a row against the cedar fence
are pruned tightly to create a
hedge that resembles espalier.
In autumn, the hornbeams'
leaves turn a bright gold.

04
A Girdle for Gravel

Welti used custom-cut steel landscape edging to
create a frame to keep gravel from migrating to
unwelcome areas; the mild steel can be bent to
create corners and curves. A similar steel lawn
edging product is widely available from landscape
supply stores; it should be installed flush with the
surface of a path to prevent a tripping hazard.

05
Let There Be Light

Scotch and Prudent strung commercial-grade
café lights in the tree branches above the dining
table. Designed for outdoor use, the lights have
encapsulated sockets with weather-resistant seals.
Globe lightbulbs are available in clear glass or
colors (including white, as shown). A waterproof
digital timer can be set to turn the lights on and off
automatically.

An Architect's Manicured Village Garden

When Barbara Chambers designed a Northern California house for herself and her husband, Guy, she thought first about what the garden needed—and made the house a supporting player.

OPPOSITE: Visible from the gravel parking area in front of the house: Barbara Chambers's love of symmetry. Twin arbutus trees flank a garage entryway, but the main garden (and the house's front door) is reached by a side path, sited to ensure that the garden beds will enjoy a southern exposure.

Architect Barbara Chambers is a self-professed perfectionist. "It's hard to control everything," she says, "especially outdoors. But I still try."

After she and her husband, Guy, bought an empty lot in Mill Valley, California, she walked around the property to figure out the best spot to build a house. The decision: she sited the house sideways to suit the garden. With a front door that faces the neighbors' property (rather than the street), the living room has windows with southern exposures, and the garden enjoys full sun all day. "All houses should be oriented this way if possible, because it gives you the best light," says Chambers. "With western exposures, you can't control the light. With east, you get light only in the morning."

Symmetry is her guiding principle. Inside the house (completed in 2013), identical doorways at opposite ends of a room echo each other. Outdoors, pathways run between mirror-image garden beds. On a patio, two lounge chairs, twin planters, and carbon-copy topiaries define the space. As a lover of classic French and English gardens, she imposes a sense of order and precision onto a landscape's design. "My garden is an architect's dream," she says. "It's all straight lines that form beautiful spaces and also complement the interior architecture of the house."

Chambers believes every window in a house should have an "axial relationship" to an outdoor view of a space defined by structure: a courtyard, path, fence, or hedge. Further, a window's special view should be precisely centered on that particular window.

In the garden, she pared down the color palette to the essentials. The predominant color is green, with white flowers such as peonies and clematis blooming seasonally, in succession. Texture, height, and shape of plants create structure and focal points. She couldn't bear the idea of a high-maintenance lawn, with willful turf that turns brown, gets bare patches, or harbors weeds. Instead she installed a green, and serene, carpet of artificial grass that, even when you are standing on it, looks completely real.

The Layered Look

Beyond the gate, a garden path leads to the front door. On both sides of the gate, pittosporum shrubs, small lavenders, olives, and boxwood are planted closely and require regular trimming to keep them from invading one another's territory. Jasmine on the wire fence creates a hedge; a row of small white myrtle trees urges the eye to look beyond the vines. The gravel is decomposed granite, mixed with a little bluestone to blend in with the garden paths (bluestone pavers cut to size by a local vendor).

No Weeds Allowed

A wire fence at lower right, lined with Carolina laurel, creates a defined space in the front garden. Simple copper caps on the fence posts offset the utilitarian look. Carefully arranged plants include clipped balls of pittosporum, lavender, peonies, olives, and boxwood; the latter will grow into a hedge.

01 Sit a Spell

Chambers put a courtyard for two opposite the house's entrance, shielded from street view by a privacy screen of Carolina laurel. The intimate space is furnished with lounge chairs and a side table from Janus et Cie's Milan collection, with aluminum frames and weather-resistant fabric.

02 Symmetry Rules

"I always do something special for a front door," says Chambers. "I generally paint them red, blue, or green, but I found some old boards of pitted oak and started to think about how I could use them." The result: an 8-foot-tall custom Dutch door (the top is often left open to frame a view of the garden). She ordered the hand-forged door knocker from Bouvet, an old French company that also supplied the door handle and the *clavos*, nails traditionally used to hold a door together (in this case they're purely decorative).

03

03 No-Mow Zone

Visitors are always surprised to learn that the lawn isn't real grass. Due to a statewide water shortage, grass is now "pretty much outlawed" in Mill Valley—new projects may have no more than 500 square feet. Chambers researched hundreds of samples before finding this realistic-looking ForeverLawn, made by DuPont. "It's expensive, but not as much as replacing real grass every two years. And when people see it, they all say, 'This is beautiful.'" Among the plants in the border are olive trees trained as shrubs, boxwood, lamb's ear, and a rosemary hedge.

04 The View Around Back

Given Chambers's commitment to symmetry, it should come as no surprise that the garden's eight Japanese maple trees march in alignment. While green and white predominate in the summer, she didn't hesitate to introduce some color to brighten the darker seasons: the maples turn a brilliant red in autumn before dropping their leaves.

04

Still Life with Coco
Chambers with the family poodle, Coco, in the outdoor dining room. Like the furniture in the front yard, the benches and table are covered in Janusfiber and can be left outside year-round. From the Janus et Cie collection the Narrows, the table is true to its name at a width of 2 feet (ideal for a constricted space).

Steal This Look

AN ARCHITECT'S DETAILS

01
Side Show

In a vestibule, bluestone pavers—the same as those used on the garden paths—create a transitional zone from outdoors to indoors. Hardware is the focus: door handles are from Bouvet, as are the custom-made "308" address numbers. The sconce is from Aldo Bernardi.

02
The Accidental Doormat

Those mats in the vestibule started life as part of the lawn. When installers were laying the artificial turf (DuPont's ForeverLawn), they cut a series of rectangular holes so they could inset paving stones to define a path across the lawn. "It wasn't planned," says Chambers, "but I just started using the cutouts for doormats and found they worked really well." Bonus: if these ever wear out, she has more stored away.

03
No Rush

Though it's only two years old, this garden looks mature thanks to the mild Mediterranean climate of Northern California. But some plants take their time: the clematis vines, intended to frame the front entryway, are slowly making their way up the wall, attached to twine. A newly planted clematis takes several years to mature, but once established in a sunny, well-drained spot like this, it will produce a profusion of exotic blossoms—in this case, white.

04
Full Disclosure

Terra-cotta planters with an agreeable patina of age are planted with annuals in a range of colors, heights, and textures. But for a perfectionist, maintaining the right look requires constant vigilance. When we checked back with Chambers a couple of months after visiting her garden, she reported: "I was going to the nursery every two weeks to replenish the plants. Eventually I got tired of that, so I've since replaced them with boxwood balls."

05
Serenity Reigns

An Aldo Bernardi sconce graces an exterior wall; the clapboard siding is painted in one of Chambers's go-to colors, New White from Farrow & Ball.

Sheltered by Live Oaks

In Austin, Texas, landscape architect Christine Ten Eyck united the microclimates surrounding her house, relying on drought-tolerant native plants in both full sun and in the deep shade beneath massive live oaks.

OPPOSITE: On the front-yard path that used to be an asphalt driveway, pea gravel covers an underlayer of stabilized decomposed granite (call it DG, as Ten Eyck does, if you want to sound in the know). Ten Eyck and her husband, Gary Deaver, brought in the big ledge stones needed to build the check dams; they repurposed smaller ledge stones that were previously part of the terrace to support more grade. Low-growing understory plants make the yard look like a forest.

When a real estate agent showed them a place on a street called Bridle Path, Christine Ten Eyck and her husband, Gary Deaver, loved the narrow residential road sheltered by enormous trees. And she was particularly struck by a majestic live oak that dominated the front yard of the property. Anybody would be.

But to the trained eye of Ten Eyck, a Phoenix-based landscape architect with plans to relocate and open a new office in Austin, the garden also offered an opportunity. The property's microclimates—shade here, blazing hot sun there, and dry, dry, dry everywhere—offered a challenge. "In Arizona, I'd learned a lot about working in arid climates," she says. In Texas, she wanted to transform a space into a serene, welcoming garden she could show potential clients to alleviate fears that she'd "try to turn their place into a desert."

After moving in, the couple first remodeled a studio to create Ten Eyck's office while taking time to get to know the garden. Although Austin gets much more rain than Phoenix (an average of 35 inches a year instead of a measly 8), Ten Eyck soon realized that water conservation remained a major concern: "My garden has only a thin crust of soil over the limestone, and the stone sucks up water like a sponge." Rainwater never puddled; it just disappeared.

To work with the climate, Ten Eyck and Deaver (a retired real estate developer who's remarkably handy in the garden) built a water-conserving courtyard fountain, planted low-water natives, and replaced both a high-maintenance lawn of turf grass and a huge circular asphalt driveway with pea gravel from Texas's Colorado River. The house sits about 8 feet higher than street level on the property's sloped lot, so Ten Eyck borrowed an ancient farming technique to create a series of "check dams," using small terraces to slow the absorption of rainwater. Hers have limestone ledges (many of the stones were found on-site) and help rain percolate into the soil to irrigate surrounding trees.

These days, the house is hidden from the street. To reach it, visitors meander along a permeable path of decomposed granite through a garden of low-water native plantings (including many varieties of agaves). In contrast to the front garden, more formal beds surround the sides and back of the house. And the massive live oak in the front yard still welcomes visitors.

Ring of Fire

A fireplace creates a destination in the side garden, which is enclosed by a stone wall. (There was a fireplace here when they bought the house, but Ten Eyck says it was "ugly as sin." The replacement is faced with stone to match the simple lines of the house, and has a steel hearth filled with soil and a layer of pea gravel.) The furniture—Munder-Skiles's classic Swan lounge chairs and matching ottomans—turns the space into an outdoor room.

Easy Fix

Replacing what Ten Eyck calls "the cruddy stone veneer" on the house's exterior walls was too big a project to undertake. Instead, she and Deaver simply changed the dark-gray color of the mortar between the stones, making the walls look more uniform. The technique, called "parging," involves covering the joints with a thin coat of mortar (in this case cream-colored) and sponging over it to smooth the surface. Around the tree they planted Texas sedge, which thrives in dry shade and is a good turf substitute.

Follow the Sun

A sunny spot in the front yard has been given over to a vegetable garden, slightly raised from the path and edged in stones. Ten Eyck, who likes to cook, harvests fresh asparagus, arugula, kale, and mustard greens, as well as herbs: parsley, cilantro, dill, creeping thyme, rosemary, and lemongrass. Among the shrubs on the left are Texas persimmon, Mexican plum, and bamboo muhly, a native grass that can grow to a height of 4½ feet.

01 Facade Face-lift

To create an attractive backdrop for the garden, Deaver restored the original steel windows to working condition and, after much testing, painted them Sherwin-Williams's Cityscape. Echoing the metal windows are the broad steps, formed by half-inch-thick steel strips—which Ten Eyck prefers to stone because of their thinner profile, "like a blade."

02 Stepping-stones

Hefty 4-inch-thick paving stones, each 48 by 28 inches, define the entrance to the house. Cast in place, the concrete was given an acid wash to eliminate the product's usual pasty gray color. (Acid-washing exposes the sand in the mix, adding texture and making the pavers less slippery when wet.) Growing beside the stone is Texas sedge.

04

05

03   Year-round Lounge

Concrete pavers lead to the side garden with a fireplace, past a sitting area with classic butterfly chairs. The chairs, whose design dates to 1938, are from Circa50; the company sells these made-to-order vinyl mesh covers in a dozen colors, and they last forever—even when the chairs stay outside year-round.

04   Heavy Metal

A wooden gate once guarded the entrance to the side garden, but Ten Eyck and Deaver replaced it with McNichols steel mesh (the same material used for fencing elsewhere on the property). Unlike solid wood, it allows sunlight to enter the garden while preventing the escape of Daisy, their basset hound–dachshund mix. The custom-made handle has rusted over time to match the gate.

05   The Unfluffy Fig

Ten Eyck encourages the creeping fig vine on the front wall of the house. "It's like an ivy, but you just need to trim it a couple times a year," she says. "Because it grows tight to the wall, and isn't fluffy, it makes the wall look like a hedge." The bench is from the Conran Shop.

Café Seating

Looking both modern and industrial, these iconic Tolix Marais A café chairs are from Design Within Reach; they are made in France from galvanized steel and have drainage holes so rainwater won't pool in the seats.

Full Circle

In the style of Spain's Moorish gardens, a brimming fountain uses just a little water to great effect. The simple trough cast in board-formed concrete allows water to spill over the sides, where it appears to run into the ground. But a perforated aluminum grate that surrounds the fountain, hidden by a layer of pea gravel, captures the water for recirculation. Growing in the pool: water lilies, blue flag iris, and black elephant ears.

Steal This Look
MANAGING MICROCLIMATES

01
Outdoor Pots

Ten Eyck adds a dash of green to the courtyard with potted plants: *Agave victoriae-reginae*, *Agave salmiana*, tradescantia, monkey tails, and sedums. To aid drainage, she places the pots directly on the gravel, and avoids overwatering.

02
Rakes' Progress

Live oaks are always dropping something, Ten Eyck says, whether it's leaves, or pollen, or acorns. She believes in the perfect tool for a job; the rake in the middle can remove debris from the base of plants without disturbing their leaves. To rake debris from gravel paths, she also has superlight aluminum rakes from Fiskars in two sizes, one 24 inches wide for raking large areas and a smaller 8-inch-wide shrub rake for tight places: "We both actually like raking—smoothing things out, tidying up, making patterns. It's very meditative."

03
Stylish Storage

"These days, all kinds of places do laser-cut steel," says Ten Eyck. "You can have it done in any design you want." The address plate sits in a spot that's easily seen from the street, but there's another reason for its location—the custom-made metal box beneath the house numbers hides an unsightly water valve.

04
Traveling Stone

This millstone, which Ten Eyck believes originally came from Bali, is a garden element she couldn't bear to leave behind in Phoenix. She got it from a developer who wasn't able to use it for a hotel project in Scottsdale. Despite its weight, the stone is easy to move if rolled. Here, it's positioned atop a rusted pipe, filled with soil and a sharkskin agave.

05
Sculptural Plants

Specimen succulents such as this *Agave salmiana* can be the stars of the show. Ten Eyck left most of the property's massive agaves in place, including an *Agave franzosinii* that's said to be the biggest in Austin. And should she want more agave, the plants are easily divided: small "pups" with roots are found around the base of the main plant. Wiggle the pups to separate the roots (watch out for spines), and transplant them to their own growing space.

A Classic Cape Cod Garden

At the heart of Sheila Bonnell and Moncrieff Cochran's garden are vegetables and herbs, given pride of place on the property's sunniest, most protected spot—the middle of the lawn. Dotted around the property are other destinations used year-round: a sauna, an outdoor shower, a toolshed, and a grassy path to the beach.

OPPOSITE: To fortify the garden against hungry marauders, Cochran bought a gate from a fence company, suspended it from two posts, and painted everything to match the house's exterior (Benjamin Moore's MoorGlo Regal Exterior White). "We added stepping-stones in front of the gate to discourage critters from sneaking underneath," says Bonnell.

When Cape Cod architect Sheila Bonnell designed her house in South Orleans, Massachusetts, she embraced the local vernacular: white clapboard siding, a peaked cedar-shingled roof, and breezy porches. "I had to see what the house and decks created before I designed the garden," she said.

Having grown up on Cape Cod, Bonnell remembered summers spent in her grandfather's big vegetable garden. But since those days, she'd lived in cities; designing a garden was a new endeavor. One thing she knew: the edible garden needed to be an extension of the house, not a plot hidden away on the property. This is how the fenced vegetable garden came to dominate the middle of the lawn, where it's convenient to the kitchen and a focal point of the landscape. Former city dweller Bonnell enjoys being grounded. "I want to be connected to the soil; I don't like being up in the air. Here, the barriers between outdoors and indoors disappear, especially in summer."

The apple tree in the middle of the garden was a must. "I associate apple trees with a sense of comfort and familiarity that's very much part of the Cape vocabulary," says Bonnell. "For me, they're gentle. Whenever you stumble upon the foundation of an old farmhouse in the woods, you always find ancient lilacs and apple trees next to it."

Around the property are other protected spaces that capture the sunlight or the summer breezes at different times of day. A covered porch and Adirondack chairs on the lawn are destinations, Bonnell says, good spots to share a glass of wine with friends. A sauna (sited not far from the master bedroom) sees year-round use.

Bonnell and her husband, Mon (short for Moncrieff) Cochran, devise their summer menus from their harvest: cherry tomatoes, lettuces, cucumbers, and herbs like tarragon, lemon thyme, and basil. She's also tried growing corn and squash—"Each year is an experiment."

Center of Attention

Bonnell and Cochran sited the edible garden between two ells of the house, where the white clapboard walls catch and reflect the sun. "In late afternoon," Bonnell says, "the whole garden is full of light." The facade of the house shelters the garden from ocean winds and salt spray.

Classic Seating

Twin Adirondack chairs are positioned to catch the sun and a garden view. They're painted the same shade of yellow as the exterior doors on the house and shed: Benjamin Moore's MoorGlo Luminous Days.

01 The Shell Game

On the west side of Orleans, a ten-minute drive from the house, sand flats stretch out as far as a mile from shore. Bonnell can beachcomb for hours, gathering whatever catches her eye—but especially the shells of razor clams, named for their resemblance to old-fashioned straight razors. Back home, she scrubs off the dried seaweed and leaves the shells to bleach in the sun.

02 Judicious Color

Bonnell's use of color is tightly controlled: "There's no pink, and only a little blue. My husband fought to get a bright color, and yellow won out." Yellow doors and colorful nasturtiums growing in a bed (built with leftover stones from the construction of the house's indoor fireplaces) provide punctuation points.

03 Intentionally Untended

Bonnell likes nasturtiums because of their long season; on Cape Cod they bloom enthusiastically from June through September. Behind them in this raised bed: English lavender and the perennial *Crocosmia* (or montbretia) 'Sunglow', whose peppy golden-yellow blossoms arch in tall sprays.

Don't Catch a Chill

Made in the United States, the sauna's electric heating element comes from New York City–based Mr. Sauna and is protected by a grille to prevent accidental burns. The floor is made of wood slats set over a sloped concrete slab; tongue-and-groove clear western red cedar covers the walls. Bonnell and Cochran use the sauna year-round, but in winter they have to turn off the water supply to the outdoor shower—requiring a dash through the cold to reach the indoor shower for their post-sauna rinse.

High-Low Style

The sauna and an outdoor shower are in a separate structure connected to the house by the roof, in what Bonnell calls "a sort of covered pass-through." A bathroom is nearby. The shower's basic fixtures are from Home Depot, but the exposed copper pipes add a touch of glamour.

Steal This Look
RELAXED YANKEE

01
Cabin in the Woods

To customize a basic garden shed, Cochran and Bonnell worked with Pine Harbor, a Cape Cod company that specializes in wooden outbuildings. The result: a design that resonates with the house, matching paint job included.

02
Gardener's Essentials

Bonnell's must-have gardening kit includes Atlas Therma Fit work gloves (handy in cold weather, with a terry liner and a rough-textured exterior for keeping a firm grip on wet, slippery tools); Felco pruners (the only ones she'll use—"They're fabulous"); and (second from left) an adjustable Green Thumb rake ("It has a slide you can move up and down along the tines, so it closes up to about three inches wide. It's really light, and we use it all the time.").

03
Tool Storage

Inside the garden shed, Bonnell drew outlines of tool handles on a rafter to help keep everything organized. Despite this effort, she admits that tools tend to come and go, "making the rounds through family members over the years, as people borrow from one another."

04
The Accordion Hose

After enduring years of trouble with hoses ("They're messy, dirty, and heavy, and they never coil up easily," says Bonnell), she discovered the TeleBrands Pocket Hose Ultra, an expand-and-shrink model that's become her new favorite. It practically puts itself away, Bonnell notes: "I *love* mine. It weighs nothing, doesn't kink, and contracts to nothing. Plus, the fabric looks better to me than polyvinyl."

05
No Free Lunch

An inexpensive fence made of chicken wire and 4-foot metal rods surrounds the vegetable beds, and deer and rabbits have yet to encroach. Bonnell suspects that the garden's location holds marauders at bay as well; few varmints will make a raid on a garden sited so close to the house.

Color Stories

A USER'S GUIDE TO GARDEN PALETTES

In the garden, a color palette is determined by more than just the plants. Hardscape materials and natural surroundings set the stage for the flowers and foliage. For inspiration, we've rounded up seven classic case studies—from a simple white garden to drought-tolerant beds of grays and greens to a backyard kaleidoscope of color—with tips you can use to replicate the look.

A Rainbow Garden of Annuals

"A garden is more of an orchestration than anything else," says Jean Victor (author of our "Expert Advice" chapter). In the Northern California garden that she designed with her architect husband, Ken Linsteadt, colorful wildflowers, flowering herbs, and annuals undercut the precision of a classic "four-square" of mirror-image beds.

OWNERS/DESIGNERS

Jean Victor and Ken Linsteadt

OPPOSITE: Every spring, the couple sows wildflower seeds in their sloped backyard garden in Northern California. Augmented by nursery seedlings (native flowers, herbs, and cutting flowers) and aided by a temperate Mediterranean climate and full sun, zinnias, sunflowers, cosmos, nicotiana, and salvias mingle freely through summer and into autumn.

CHEAT SHEET

BEFORE YOU PLANT
*Construct symmetrical beds to calm
the impending chaos.*

HARDSCAPE MATERIAL
Elk Mountain stone
*The neutral brown tones complement
natural surroundings.*

GOOD BONES
Boxwood balls and cypress trees
*These lend architectural interest and
year-round greenery.*

COLOR WHEEL
Brightly colored annuals
*Mix-and-match flowering plants include
varieties of sunflowers, zinnias, cosmos,
nicotiana, and Mimulus cardinalis.*

BONUS
Edibles
*Interplanted with ornamentals, pumpkin
and squash vines add surprise.*

Controlled Chaos

Within a grid structure created by
retaining walls, four rectangular beds
bisected by a central staircase play
different roles: In the foreground,
perennials and roses encircle a path
of grass. On the same level, in the
background, cutting flowers behind a
low hedge of boxwood suggest a mini
wildflower meadow. Two upper-level
beds are reserved, respectively, for
edibles (including the beans on the
arbor) and for herbs such as lavender.

01 Height of Summer

The couple fearlessly mixes color. The element that unifies the riot of cosmos, marigolds, lavender, and nicotiana is a certain delicacy: ruffled blossoms, swan-neck stems, and lacy foliage. Adding structure to the wild garden are clipped boxwood balls in patio planters and pencil-thin Italian cypress trees (they line the path that bisects the garden beds).

02 Monkey Flower

Orange flowers on long stems of *Mimulus cardinalis* sway gracefully in a breeze. In temperate growing zones, these flowers will reach a height of 2 feet (cut back the stems if a plant gets too leggy) and are an excellent lure for hummingbirds. Also known as monkey flower, *Mimulus cardinalis* will thrive in sun or partial shade but prefers not to have its roots dry out (which is why you'll often see it growing along the banks of a stream).

02

03

03 Seat of Power

Along the back fence line of the property, a garden bed is reserved for the pleasure of beans, which grow on an iron arbor purchased from Cottage Gardens in Petaluma. In winter, the bare arch (which sits at the lot's highest elevation) is visible from the house and lends structure and architectural interest.

04 Hello, Sunshine

Many varieties of *Helianthus* (sunflower) mingle in the garden. Native to the United States, most widely cultivated sunflowers are annuals that will self-sow if left to their own devices at the end of the season. The couple's favorite varieties include *Helianthus annuus* 'Delta Sunflower' (deer-resistant, it attracts pollinators) and *Helianthus gracilentus* 'Slender Sunflower' (a drought-resistant California native).

04

05 A Royal Rose

'The Prince' is one of nearly two hundred varieties cultivated by the British rose breeder David Austin, known for breeding roses with old-fashioned scents and a modern proclivity to bloom repeatedly throughout a growing season. 'The Prince' is a hardy, strongly fragrant shrub rose that will produce flowers all summer if spent blooms are deadheaded properly (cut back stems to a five-leaf juncture). The color is a rich red that over time deepens to a majestic purple.

06 Tucked Away

In this garden nook, fruit trees, perennial herbs such as lavender, and a puddle of nasturtiums (in the foreground) are encouraged to grow wild, to create a screen around the seating area. A teak garden bench hidden in a corner is one of many little surprises that make the backyard appear bigger than it is.

07 White Light

Queen Anne's lace (*Daucus carota*) grows to a height of 3 feet and, thanks to its tendency to spread fast, fills in gaps other plants leave behind after they finish blooming. A good plant for pollinator gardens, it lures both butterflies and bees (and reseeds itself enthusiastically, useful to prevent a naturalistic planting scheme from looking too studied).

08 The Odd Couple

The formality of a thin, vertical Italian cypress tree is undercut with an unruly pumpkin vine that is encouraged to grow over an arbor and twine itself around the tree. Irregularly sized pavers and edging stones reinforce the idea that controlled chaos is encouraged.

A Rainbow Garden of Annuals

Color Stories

A Whiter Shade of Pale

The formality of a structured landscape—with masonry retaining walls, a bluestone terrace, a vegetable parterre, and espaliered fruit trees—sets the scene for the pared-down palette of this white garden, designed for a five-story town house in Carroll Gardens.

OWNERS
Jennifer and Benjamin Whitfield
DESIGNER
Susan Welti, Foras Studio

OPPOSITE: Four steel-sided raised beds delineate a kitchen garden along a fence line, ceding the garden's sunniest spot to vegetables and blueberry bushes. A crushed bluestone border discourages weeds and provides a neutral backdrop for white flowering plants (including hydrangeas in bloom at left) and an espaliered apple tree on the fence.

CHEAT SHEET

BEFORE YOU PLANT
*Divide your space into "rooms" to
create multiple small, controllable
environments.*

HARDSCAPE MATERIAL
Bluestone
*The cool gray tones are a classic foil
for white.*

GOOD BONES
Pleached hornbeams
*A mature row of pleached hornbeams
delineates boundaries more gracefully
than a fence.*

COLOR WHEEL
Splashes of white
*Apple blossoms, pom-pom hydrangeas,
and feathery Veronicastrum ensure white
accents from early spring through late
September.*

BONUS
Fast-growing foliage
*The vegetable garden and berry bushes
create a neutral backdrop for other
garden elements.*

01 Divide and Conquer

The garden's layout, visible from
a balcony on an upper floor of the
recently remodeled nineteenth-century
town house, divides the backyard
into four distinct spaces: a bluestone
dining terrace, an artificial grass lawn,
the kitchen garden, and a gravel patio
behind a row of pleached hornbeams
(underplanted with a yew hedge
pruned to a height of 2 feet).

02 Quick Prep

On the back side of the retaining wall is
a 4-inch-deep outdoor sink for washing
vegetables. It is fabricated of bluestone
to match an elevated drainboard. The
faucet was a find on eBay, "the best
place to look for a simple, simple little
old faucet," says Welti. "I think I paid
fifteen dollars for it."

03 Crowd-Pleaser

A clump of *Hydrangea arborescens*
'Annabelle' provides a reliable white
accent, producing summer blooms
that will last into September. Its
enormous mop-head flowers (12 inches
in diameter) and blowsy shape (the
shrub will reach a floppy height of 5
feet) have made it a favorite variety of
snowball hydrangea.

Garden to Table
Jennifer Whitfield, a trained chef, "wanted a feeling of abundance in the vegetable garden, and to really be able to work in the garden," says Welti. "Fortunately she had enough sunlight to accomplish that." Cherry tomatoes grow on a tepee trellis in the raised bed closest to the house.

04 Cherry on Top

Cherry tomatoes, which typically grow to a diameter of 2 inches, are more prolific and easier to care for than their finicky beefsteak cousins. These cherry tomatoes grow on determinate bushes (rather than indeterminate vines), need no pruning, and are a good choice for a small garden or as a container plant on a sunny balcony.

05 White on White

Strings of miniature paper lanterns, intermingled with a variegated ivy with white-edged leaves, echo the snowball hydrangea and add yet another round, white element.

06 Feathery Friend

In the back of the garden (beyond the pleached hornbeams), *Veronicastrum* grows against the fence. Known colloquially as Culver's root, it is an airy plant that lends height and interest to a small garden. Irresistible to pollinators, this native North American wildflower thrives along the East Coast in both sun and shade.

07 Box Logic

For the raised beds, 18-inch-wide lengths of steel were cut to size, then primed and painted before being buried a foot deep in the ground.

Fiery Flora in an English Cottage Garden

Classicist architect Ben Pentreath, who oversaw the interior design of the Duke and Duchess of Cambridge's twenty-room home at Kensington Palace, had something less grand in mind for himself when he obtained a long-term lease on an old parsonage in the picturesque village of Littlebredy (population: 82). With husband Charlie McCormick, he designed the colorful herbaceous borders the nineteenth-century house (and the medieval parish church next door) had deserved all along.

OWNERS/DESIGNERS

Ben Pentreath and Charlie McCormick

OPPOSITE: Pentreath annexed the movie-set facades of neighbors' cottages to use as scenic backdrops for his garden. Here in the lower garden, the look is all about symmetry: a double garden gate (purchased for £30 at an agricultural supplies store and reinforced with chicken wire); twin cottage chimneys in the distance; and a mown grass path bisecting a pair of garden beds planted with a mix of flowers (including staked dahlias, irises, and cosmos) and edibles.

CHEAT SHEET

BEFORE YOU PLANT

Improve soil by digging out weeds (and filtering the dirt to remove random roots) before digging in compost to a depth of 24 inches.

HARDSCAPE MATERIALS

Brick and woven willow fencing

A mossy patina enhances the old bricks, and the willow fencing creates a friendly backdrop.

GOOD BONES

Dry-laid stone retaining walls

The walls double as edging for garden beds.

COLOR WHEEL

Gemstone hues

Tender plants such as sweet peas, dahlias, hollyhocks, and flowering herbs thrive in a mild, temperate climate.

BONUS

Mown grass paths

Softscape in lieu of stone or another hard material is a reminder of a gentler era.

01 Dahlia Rampage

A dissection of the planting plan reveals a riotous mix: orange poppies, nasturtiums, and many preening dahlias, including varieties with flowers shaped like dinner plates, double peonies, and pom-poms. Among Pentreath's favorites are ruffled purple-and-white 'Edinburgh', spiky golden 'Glorie of Noordwijk', and velvety dark-red 'Chat Noir'. His most successful plant combinations "are entirely down to chance and luck," he says.

02 Pampering Preferred

Well-loved in England's mild, temperate climate, the decorative 'Edinburgh' dahlia is also a garden favorite at Vita Sackville-West's world-famous Sissinghurst Castle. Dahlias grow from tubers, which in cold climates should be dug up to spend the winter asleep in a bed of dry straw in the cellar.

04

03 Master Gardeners

Pentreath (at left) and his husband, Charlie McCormick, stand at the edge of the herbaceous border. Spilling over the edge and down the slope are prolific pink-and-white *Erigeron karvinskianus* (commonly known in the UK as Mexican fleabane, and in the United States as Santa Barbara daisy).

04 More to Come

A set of brick steps leads from the lower garden (where the dahlias reign) to the upper lawn, where the old parsonage sits. Flanking the stairs (and adding a sculptural element) are four clipped balls of boxwood and simple terra-cotta pots planted with herbs.

Succession Planting
A grass path between the flower beds leads to the old parsonage (built in 1820). The flower beds provide color from spring (tulips and lupines) through summer (lilies, foxgloves, and hollyhocks) and into early autumn (daisies, Japanese anemones, and more dahlias).

05

05 Garden Design

From a distance, the garden's linear layout is apparent. Placing the large garden bed in the center of the lawn gave Pentreath the ability to site the tallest plants in the center rather than at the back of the border, and to plant medium and small plants around the entire perimeter.

06 Old-Fashioned Fragrance

Growing against the facade of the house are Pentreath's favorite climbing roses, 'Mme. Alfred Carrière' (whose pink-tinged white flowers are intensely perfumed) and 'Clarence House' (a creamy white bloomer with double flowers and a sweet scent). A velvety green ribbon of low-clipped boxwood corrals the vines without competing for attention with a double-hung window.

06

Borrowed Neighbor
Pentreath's garden design incorporates the church next door. Framed by flowers, St. Michael and All Angels (with a fourteenth-century stone tower and a steeple added in the mid-1800s) appears to belong to the garden. And it does.

A Palette of Perennials Inspired by the High Line

Impressed by how well Dutch garden designer Piet Oudolf's painterly drifts of perennial plantings on the High Line Park stand up to New York City's freezing winters and summer heat, garden designer Julie Farris of XS Space planted a similarly drought- and wind-tolerant mix in her Cobble Hill roof garden.

OWNER/DESIGNER

Julie Farris, XS Space

OPPOSITE: Farris's roof garden looks like a wild meadow. Visible in this planting bed are hardy grasses (including varieties of miscanthus, calamagrostis, and nassella) interplanted with flowering asters, nepetas, agastaches, and—spilling over the edge of the bed—strawberries.

CHEAT SHEET

BEFORE YOU PLANT
Ask a structural engineer to verify that your roof can support the weight.

HARDSCAPE MATERIALS
Ipe decks and paths
This dense, durable South American hardwood will weather to a soft silvery gray.

GOOD BONES
Raised planting beds
Beds divide and define the space as "rooms" for dining, lounging, and playing.

COLOR WHEEL
Blue, pink, white, and purple perennials
Agastache (blue), monarda (pink), gaura (white), and nepeta (purple) complement one another, feed pollinators such as butterflies and bees, and return year after year.

BONUS
Artificial turf
No mowing or water is required to keep this lawn emerald green.

01   All-Weather Terrain

Farris bought rugged outdoor furniture that can stay on the roof in winter ("We don't even cover it") because, like most city dwellers, she doesn't have a shed or garage to use for storage. The stainless and teak dining table and Monterey teak outdoor sofa are from TeakWarehouse.com. Farris recommends oiling teak every year or two to keep it looking good. The dining chairs, from Crate & Barrel's Regatta Mesh collection, "are a great alternative to the mesh chairs Richard Schultz designed for Knoll if you are not up for the outlay of money."

02   What Lies Beneath

Farris installed a multilayer support system beneath a 14-inch layer of soil to improve drainage and ensure that the roof could support the added weight of a garden. Layers include a waterproof membrane, a root protection barrier, a drainage mat (from J-Drain.com), a layer of filter fabric, and a 2-inch layer of Styrofoam.

03   Hardscape Hints

The hardscape materials used by Farris include artificial turf (to create a play area for her sons), strips of ipe decking, and recessed pin lights from Jesco (JescoLighting.com). "They emit a soft white light, and spaced five feet apart and off center in an ipe walkway, they look absolutely lovely," says Farris.

02

03

A Palette of Perennials Inspired by the High Line

Color Stories

04 Disappearing Act

Hidden neatly behind a dark-stained wall are the vents, condensers, and other unsightly features typically found on a city rooftop. Also out of sight are the irrigation system's controller and electrical panels.

05 Going Native

The perennial daisy sky-blue aster (*Aster azureus*) is native to the North Atlantic region and requires little water to keep happy.

06 Water Wise

An automated irrigation system delivers water where it's needed, without waste, and for drainage, the entire roof pitches toward a downspout that flows into an underground pipe. Farris installed a filter to keep debris from clogging the pipe.

07 Prairie Effect

Planted in drifts to create a naturalistic effect, feathery white gaura, pink monarda, and perennial grasses all sway gently when they catch a rooftop breeze.

04

05

06

A Palette of Perennials Inspired by the High Line

Color Stories

Sunny Notes in a Wildflower Meadow Garden

Simple wildflowers color the luxuriant meadow surrounding the country house built in upstate New York by interior designer Lucien Rees Roberts and architect Steven Harris. The best part: no weeding required.

OWNERS/DESIGNERS

Steven Harris and Lucien Rees Roberts
(see the rest of their property on pages 82–95)

OPPOSITE: A self-sustaining meadow of wildflowers, planted on a sunny upslope that borders the lawn, blooms from late spring through early autumn thanks to a succession of native wildflowers. The only upkeep is mowing; every few weeks walkways get clipped to keep them passable.

CHEAT SHEET

BEFORE YOU PLANT

Know your soil; choose a seed mix suited to your conditions (a meadow thrives in clay soil).

HARDSCAPE MATERIAL

Mown walkway

For a natural, low-maintenance path, mow a walkway through the flowers.

GOOD BONES

Wildflowers that reseed, such as larkspur, daisies, and poppies

Sow wildflowers, such as varieties of milkweed, to support the local wildlife.

COLOR WHEEL

A yellow and white palette with complementary accents

Here, the purple hue of cow vetch heightens the effect of yellow and white daisies and clovers.

BONUS

Architectural interest of spent blooms

Allow flowers to remain in place so they can set seeds (and to feed the birds).

01   Purple Power

Adding a dash of purple to the meadow, fast-spreading cow vetch (the common name for *Vicia cracca*, a European native plant) flowers from late spring through late summer; its blooms provide nectar for bees and butterflies. After it goes to seed, it's a good source of food for local birds.

02   Volunteer Army

Wild daisies self-sow freely, spreading throughout the meadow.

03   Scattered Seeds

The meadow's naturally occurring plants get a little help every year. Garden designer David Kelly sows mixes from Pennsylvania-based Ernst Seeds, which specializes in native and heirloom varieties. Kelly buys both the company's Low-Growing Wildflower & Grass Mix (which has fifteen varieties of seeds, predominantly sheep fescue and ryegrass) and Annual Wildflower Mix (with two dozen varieties, including cosmos, flax, cornflowers, poppies, larkspur, and daisies).

01

02

04

04 Picky Eaters' Pick

Fourleaf milkweed (*Asclepias quadrifolia*), native to the eastern United States, thrives on sunny upland slopes. The foliage of milkweeds is an essential source of food for caterpillars of the monarch butterfly.

05 A Sunny Show

This fast-spreading yellow wildflower is wild indigo (*Baptisia tinctoria*), an East Coast native that thrives in full sun and well-drained soil.

06 Waves of Grass

The wildflower meadow extends to the banks of one of the property's ponds, where yellow baptisia and purple vetch (visible in the foreground) mingle with taller grasses to create a fringed border that sways gently in a breeze.

05

Woodland Hues in a Shade Garden

Sited in a canyon and overshadowed by giant redwoods, a Northern California garden relies on dappled sunlight and foliage—purple, burgundy, and red leaves—to create a colorful miniature forest.

LANDSCAPE ARCHITECT

J.C. Miller of Miller Studio Landscape Architecture

OPPOSITE: Bluestone pavers set in sand (instead of mortar) create a permeable patio that filters rainwater and prevents run-off in the sun-dappled side yard. Bordering the seating area is a low hedge of *Loropetalum chinense* (commonly known as fringe flower). Alongside the house grows *Asarum canadense* (wild ginger), a dense green carpet that connects the stone visually to the facade.

CHEAT SHEET

BEFORE YOU PLANT
Assess the light; lay out rambling paths
to pass through a shade garden's sunniest
spots.

HARDSCAPE MATERIALS
Natural wood planks (for fences and
gates) and cedar mulch
Neutral hardscape elements recede into
the background to heighten the colors of
surrounding foliage.

GOOD BONES
Judiciously pruned trees
Trim existing trees to coax more filtered
light (and warmth) into a wooded garden.

COLOR WHEEL
Plants with purple and deep
red leaves
Heucheras and loropetalums will look
especially rich against a silvery green
backdrop.

BONUS
A private patio
Surrounded by trees and greenery,
patios feel secluded even when they're
near the house.

02

01 The Silver Screen

Behind landscape architect J. C. Miller, a screen of small-leaved shrubbery—*Pittosporum tenuifolium* 'Silver Sheen'—grows in freeform waves. Rather than shaping the bushes into a row of tightly clipped forms (as is more typical), Miller allows the silvery fronds "to jump back and forth in the wind."

02 Lawn Substitute

The environmentally conscious owners wanted a garden that could be maintained without chemicals or use of a power mower. Clumps of ajuga, mulched with cedar chips to discourage weeds, replace a traditional turf grass lawn.

The Undowdy Dowager

The Dutch Colonial–style house was built in the 1920s, but the owners prefer a contemporary style and simplified the entryway by replacing an old-fashioned front stoop with pre-cast concrete pavers. To impose a modern sensibility on a traditional garden, "you want to prune judiciously, so the look of trees and shrubs is loose, almost transparent," says Miller. "It creates a vibe that's not super formal, but still clearly tailored."

03 Accent Colors

Made of lightweight, pre-cast concrete, a patio planter creates a striking color story with contrasting foliage: silvery green succulents, burgundy-colored *Oxalis vulcanicola* 'Zinfandel' (with small yellow flowers), purple alyssum, and a spray of spiky grasses.

04 Lilliputian Charm

Aptly nicknamed dollhouse fern, low-growing *Cotula leptinella* 'Platt's Black' has foliage with a purple sheen (and looks darker in sunlight). It grows densely and has a shallow root system, which makes it ideally suited to creeping between stones to fill cracks with a velvety carpet.

05 Circular Thinking

A self-coiling hose lives inside a low, round bowl when not in use. Made in Oregon by Water Right Inc., the accordion hose expands to a length of 75 feet and retracts to a length of 60 inches.

06 Watercolor World

Reclaimed cobblestones (found on the property by the owners) are used for an informal stepping-stone path through the garden. The purple foliage of ajuga and dollhouse fern groundcovers blends together into a watercolor backdrop for the gray stones.

The Many Shades of Desert Green

Inspired by the palette (and low water requirements) of the nearby desert, garden designer Judy Kameon planted a remarkably lush mix of blue, gray, and green hues in a small courtyard garden in Los Angeles.

OWNER

Isabel Marant

DESIGNER

Judy Kameon, Elysian Landscapes

OPPOSITE: Kameon designed the garden to appear, at sunrise, as a "chromatic and textural study, with a shift from dark-green, leafy edges toward a more static, sculptural center of light greens and ivory." The garden's margins recede, focusing attention on the early morning dappled sunlight that hits the *Lophocereus schottii monstrose* (totem pole cactus) and *Kalanchoe beharensis* succulents.

CHEAT SHEET

BEFORE YOU PLANT
Install a drip irrigation system to deliver water precisely, as needed, to roots of trees, shrubbery, and other nondesert plants.

HARDSCAPE MATERIALS
Mexican pea gravel, flagstone, and bluestone
Shades of blue and gray stones blend together into a uniform backdrop for plants.

GOOD BONES
Totem pole cacti
Mature specimen plants add height and drama to a low-growing succulents garden.

COLOR WHEEL
Blues and greens with a dash of orange
The blooms of bird of paradise plants add a warm, tropical note to the cool palette.

BONUS
Year-round greenery
Evergreen and low-maintenance, succulents and cacti will be colorful even in winter.

01   Molten Moments

In the foreground, an Agave 'Blue Flame' lives up to its name as it catches the light; in the background, the orange flowers of *Strelitzia reginae* (bird of paradise plant) add another dash of fiery color.

02   Picture Perfect

Inspired by the candelabra shapes of existing trees—a mature olive (left) and Chinese elm (right)—Kameon designed a sidewalk view to frame the front windows. Adding additional vertical emphasis, the totem pole cacti draw the eye up into the leafy canopies of the trees.

03   Playing the Blues

Cool-toned Mexican gravel is used throughout the garden to tie the planting beds to the foot paths. The gray pebbles provide a subtle contrast to the blue-green and gray-blue leaves of the succulents.

Center of Attention
Beneath a Chinese elm tree, a creamy variegated agave holds court, surrounded by blue- and gray-leaved succulents that serve as a foil for its bright ivory and chartreuse leaves.

04 Blue Beauty
Blue aeoniums grow in clusters, with small rosettes springing up to surround a central clump.

05 Special Specimens
The cool tones and rounded shape of Mexican pea gravel complement the blue-green leaves of Agave *parryi ssp. truncata*. Native to Mexico and often described as "the most beautiful succulent of all," the plant grows to a diameter of 18 inches with perfectly symmetrical leaves in a rounded ball shape.

06 Foundation Plantings
With its circular structure of leaves, an Agave 'Blue Flame' is a compact rosette, edging the path that leads to the front door; at full size it may grow to a diameter of up to 3 feet. Similar agaves are scattered throughout the garden for repetition; beneath them grow purple-tinged *Aeonium hawortii*.

Annexing the Outdoors

EIGHT CREATIVE WAYS TO GET MORE
FROM YOUR GARDEN

*Yes, the garden is for gardening. But it's also for
meeting, cooking, camping, farming, and playing, among
other critical activities. Here, we share eight inspired
and inspiring case studies of hardworking gardens that,
with ingenious outbuildings and enclosures, bring more
life out of doors.*

By Jessica Marshall

A Modernist Outdoor Kitchen

Dutch designer Piet-Jan van den Kommer and his business partner, Martijn Vree, have created a thriving enterprise around a streamlined design for a plein air kitchen that will withstand the elements in striking modern style.

DESIGNERS

Piet-Jan van den Kommer and Martijn Vree, WWOO

OPPOSITE: Van den Kommer was already well known in Europe for his wood, stone, and concrete interiors when he decided he couldn't stomach the high-cost, low-durability, and fundamentally fussy outdoor kitchens he'd seen. An entrepreneur since childhood, van den Kommer created a prototype for a modular outdoor kitchen using his favorite materials, and secured a patent and a partner, Martijn Vree. WWOO—now available in thirteen countries around the world (although, sadly, not the United States)—was born.

01

01 And the Kitchen Sink

Although it looks custom when assembled, a WWOO kitchen is actually multiple anthracite or light-gray concrete units, each 1½ meters wide, and an array of add-ons. "You can get as much or as little as you want," says Vree. For example, you might want WWOO's communal table, here in kiln-dried oak, and a set of matching chairs. You might also want WWOO's canopy and cement pavers. It's addictive.

02 Set Sails

The supports for WWOO's sailcloth canopies are made of beechwood baked until it has the qualities of hardwood.

03 The Incredible Egg

The ceramic Big Green Egg, an updated Japanese kamado grill, allows for precise temperature control as well as good old American charring. WWOO has no qualms about declaring the Big Green Egg the "best outdoor cooker available" and shaping the firm's concrete shelving around it. Unconvinced? A tabletop grill will also fit the setup. Ample storage space for hardwood and charcoal is provided.

02

03

04

04 Concrete Plans

Concrete pavers allow outdoor furniture the greatest chance of even footing—and strike a contrast with the reclaimed bricks (Dutch, in this instance) used in the interstices.

05 Tidy Tricks

WWOO uses custom wooden boxes as camouflage for the sink basin as well as for storage drawers. On deck are a Redecker dish brush in untreated beechwood and copper pot scrubbers (ideal for cleaning steel sinks without scratching).

06 Practical Plumbing

The stainless-steel WWOO sink, whose faucet recalls our favorite Chicago Faucets rigid gooseneck spout, is designed to connect to a garden hose.

07 Bravo, Mother Nature

The quiet palette and modest lines of the WWOO kitchen allow the colors and accidental shapes of natural phenomena to look as extraordinary as they are. Just steps from the kitchen, an apple tree steals the show.

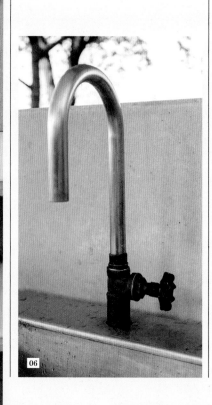

06

05

LOS ANGELES, CALIFORNIA

A Backyard Playground

When an LA family wanted a children's garden to complement their Asian-style house, their designers at trendsetting Commune Design contacted Matthew Brown. Best known for his landscape work for the ACE hotels, Brown was more than game. Drawing inspiration from the bohemian play spaces of his LA childhood, he created a shaded oasis as inviting for children as it is relaxing for adults.

DESIGNERS

Commune Design

LANDSCAPE DESIGNER

Matthew Brown

OPPOSITE: Chinese elms, with sinuous limbs that evoke the spirit of the house, filter the sunlight that falls on a handmade gaga pit. Gaga, dubbed a "gentler version of dodgeball," is said to have made its way to the States from Israel via Jewish day camps (*ga-ga* is Hebrew for touch-touch).

02

01   Quirky Contemporary

Brown paired plants he found on-site with an offbeat combination of new plants from his "rescue nursery" in the hills above Los Feliz. (If you're not near enough to visit, create your own collection of unexpected vegetation by following Brown's credo: "When walking nurseries, go to the outer edges and peek behind fences and gates—that is where all the treasures are.") The look he's after: "A bit of an 'island of misfit plants' that over time achieves a unique look and integrity." Here, drought-resistant pink cane begonias leap out from a multitextured sea of greens lining a pathway of Del Rio gravel in ¼-inch to ⅝-inch stones.

02   Got That Swing

The land falls steeply away from the yard, providing an engrossing view for a vintage toddler swing. Although the children's gardens and the adult spaces are separate, Brown says, "There are visual overlaps, as each would love to experience the other's world."

03   Hammock at Work

The elevation of the yard was raised 4 feet to add a flat playing area that Brown covered with Marathon fescue lawn, adding fern pines for privacy and more Asiatic notes. Chinese elms provide sturdy anchor points for a classic Pawleys Island hammock, suitable for swinging children in bulk or rocking adults one by one.

03

04   All in the Picking

A piece of a demolished fountain from the front of the house welcomes walkers to the lower garden. Quirky grace notes collected from unusual sources are a hallmark of Brown's style. His advice: "Never feel ashamed stopping on the side of the road and peeking in a Dumpster or trash can; picking is a satisfying lifestyle."

05   Jungle Gym

A sapote tree, common in Mexico, supports a rope swing ready to launch riders into the greenery. The especially irregular stepping-stones are red Colorado sandstone, worn to smoothness.

Burnt Offerings

To complement the 1920s stucco house, designers at Commune Design came up with the idea of an elongated outdoor fireplace as a focal point for a deck. With proportions that trick the eye (including a squat firebox and a generously chunky hearth), the 13-foot chimney rises like a fairy-tale beanstalk toward the sky, creating a sense of spaciousness. A pair of low-slung rocking chairs, sourced at Blackman Cruz in LA, further emphasize the height.

A Summery Screened Porch

A nineteenth-century barn on Cape Cod has a new life as a studio and bedroom, thanks to a pair of barn doors that inspired owner Miranda Heller to design a screened-porch addition. The doors roll away to create a cooling cross breeze even at the height of summer.

OWNER
Miranda Heller

OPPOSITE: From a distance, the screened porch appears to have always been there, attached to the side of the barn. "The question was: how do you structurally follow the peaked line of the barn's roof?" says Heller. "We decided to build out the porch roof at the same angle, so it's seamless."

01 Barn Dance

When fully open, the doors create a 15-foot-wide entrance into the old barn. Built in the early 1800s, the barn was moved uphill to its current site by former owners Lucy and William L'Engle. They were twentieth-century Expressionist painters who kept the barn as a studio and "used to throw huge parties in it for theater people, including Eugene O'Neill," says Heller. "But the barn is up against the tree line, and on the Cape that means mosquitoes—you just couldn't ever have the door open without a screen."

02 Garden to Vase

A French enamel vase, a flea-market find, displays a few stems of bright orange crocosmias (which bloom from midsummer to fall).

03 Simple Shelves

Heller collects seashells from the beach down the road; the porch's framing doubles as a narrow display shelf.

Family Affair

The new porch's simple timber skeleton is an homage to a nearby house that Heller's grandfather, the self-taught modernist architect Jack Phillips, built from salvaged army barracks in the 1940s. "It was one of the houses I grew up in, with a simple, squared-out porch, where the framing also can be used as windowsills and shelves; you can put a book or a glass on it," says Heller. "It's kind of genius, and I wanted to copy his idea."

04

05

04 Scandi Style

Complementing the simple rusticity of the exposed ceiling beams, this IKEA Leran pendant has a handmade woven bamboo shade.

05 Form as Function

The porch's graceful proportions would have pleased Heller's grandfather, who chose the most minimal building materials available and favored the slender profile of 2-by-3 lengths of lumber over chunkier wood profiles. On Heller's porch, screens are stapled onto the exterior facade; staples are hidden under thin strips of wood. "If the screens tear, you just unscrew the strips of wood and put in a new screen," she says.

06

06 Raise High the Roof Beams
Seen through the windows between the porch and barn, Heller vacuums in the barn. "You can see the beams and the construction of the barn are exposed—it's one of the things I love about the barn, and I wanted the same rawness and squared-out structure when we built the porch," she says.

07 Mossy Moment
On the lawn, vintage wooden garden furniture complements the rusticity of the barn and screened porch. "Everybody is always telling me to get rid of the old furniture, but instead I keep rebuilding it because I love it so much," says Heller.

08 Skylight
The porch was built against the barn's north-facing wall, where small windows still get ample sunlight thanks to the installation of a Plexiglas skylight.

07

08

The Eat-In Kitchen Garden

Former singer-songwriter Lauri Kranz, the founder of
Edible Gardens LA, has made a specialty of creating delightful,
easy-care kitchen gardens for clients who are ready to get their
hands dirty. Guests welcome—unless you're a deer.

DESIGNER
Lauri Kranz, Edible Gardens LA

OPPOSITE: Asked to design and build a kitchen garden on a Bel
Air estate's park-like grounds, Kranz produced a tall, slim structure
decked in hardware cloth. "The screens are large enough to let the
bees and butterflies in but small enough to keep rodents, squirrels,
and raccoons out."

Magic Wand
LA residents have called Kranz their "fairy godmother of gardening." Self-taught, she eases others' transition from black- to green-thumb status by planting hardy herbs and low-maintenance edible plants. A lemon-filled cerulean ceramic bowl by local potter Victoria Morris for Edible Gardens LA adorns one of the built-in benches.

01 Breakfast Nook

Brimming with plants, the garden enclosure appears spacious and inviting thanks to its 8-foot walls. Breakfast is served on an antique French café table with weathered chairs. (IKEA's Tarno bistro set in acacia wood would be a serviceable substitute.)

02 Framing

One-by-ones cover sharp metal edges while holding screens in place. Kranz stained the wood olive green to blend in with the surroundings—but has also been known to choose a bold modernist black.

03 Making Beds

Kranz uses untreated redwood or cedar for her raised beds, which range from 18 to 24 inches high with a minimum space of 24 inches between each row. Pea gravel ensures a mud-free path—these gardens provide food come rain or shine.

The Eat-In Kitchen Garden

Annexing the Outdoors

04 Tomato Season

Easygoing cherry tomatoes have a longer season than beefsteaks and produce fruit reliably until the first frost. The fruit of the Indigo Apple tomato (available from Baker Creek Heirloom Seeds) starts black and lightens to red at maturity.

05 Opportunists

Tomatoes take advantage of the garden's screen to climb toward the sun, and last well into the fall.

06 Orderly Conduct

Beans are trained onto a compact tepee to minimize the shade they'll throw as they grow.

07 Subversive Details

A concrete urn, one of Kranz's vintage finds, provides a sly reference within the modesty of the garden to the grandeur of the surrounding estate.

MILL VALLEY, CALIFORNIA

A Yoga Studio in the Redwoods

Start with a stand of coast redwoods, among the tallest and oldest plants on Earth. Now add a yoga studio—without disturbing their grandeur. This outbuilding in Northern California proves it's possible.

OWNER

Kathy Sloan

ARCHITECT

Jonathan Feldman, Feldman Architecture

LANDSCAPE ARCHITECT

Jori Hook

OPPOSITE: The studio, sited a few hundred feet from the main house, seems as if it's in another world. It blends into the natural surroundings with walls made of hardy cedar covered with a preweathered stain, providing patina and protection. Boston ivy and creeping ficus climb up the exterior—the ficus requires trimming a few times a year to keep it from getting bushy.

Roof Raising

The design team thought a roof garden tucked into the hillside would provide owner Kathy Sloan, an avid gardener, with a new gardening experience: "You don't need a ladder or special rock-climbing skills. You just have to hop on," says landscape architect Jori Hook. The studio's structure was specially reinforced to support the weight of the plants as well as a lightweight, pumice-based soil mix 5 inches deep.

01

01 Pearly Greens

The centerpiece of the roof garden is a thick stripe of densely clumped *Echeveria albicans*. The silvery plant stays compact as it offsets, making it ideal for low-maintenance, high-impact planting.

02 Making Waves

After laying down 5 inches of a pumice and red lava rock soil mix, Hook and Sloan chose succulents in various textures and tones from Succulent Gardens in Castroville, California, to create an undulating pattern. The partially shaded setting is ideal for succulents: "Everyone thinks succulents like full sun all the time, but they actually prefer less sun," says Feldman. "They don't tell you they're stressed until it's too late."

03 The Journey

The path from the house to the studio meanders along a deliberately indirect route, with views that urge walkers to stop and take it all in from strategically placed benches.

A Yoga Studio in the Redwoods

Annexing the Outdoors

04 Ascension

Stairs made of redwood and blocks of local stone give the impression of being hand-hewn. A clump of purple pelargoniums at the base of the stairs adds a moment of color. "Everything here emphasizes the journey from house to studio and is designed to make that journey enjoyable," says Hook.

05 Faux Originals

Boulders of local serpentine rock were used as stepping-stones. "The idea is that the steps look as if they came out of the mountain itself," says Feldman. Although the designers chose primarily native plants, one import that has done particularly well is 'Catlin's Giant'—a variety of ajuga, from the mint family. Spikes of its purple flowers jut up between stones.

06 Illumination

To avoid the landing-strip look, discreet copper pathway lights are placed at irregular intervals to encourage residents to take the walk from house to studio at night as well as during the day.

Glamping Guest Quarters

When Jennifer Moses and Ron Beller transplanted themselves to Northern California from London and discovered that the best views on their Napa getaway property could be enjoyed only from nearly unbuildable hillsides, they were undaunted. Taking a page from luxury safaris, the couple created an outdoor retreat that makes full use of the stunning surroundings.

OWNERS/DESIGNERS

Jennifer Moses and Ron Beller

OPPOSITE: After taking sleeping bags up to the ridge to catch the sunrise, the couple began to look for high-quality tents that would let them spend the night in style. A local carpenter made oversized redwood platforms, and a year-round glamping site was born. High-end furnishings mix with bargains: lovely yet durable vintage Turkish rugs from Summer House in nearby Mill Valley; hand-wrought iron lanterns from Mexico-based Casamidy, and shearling throws from IKEA. The Estancia butterfly chair with a natural linen cover and suede backing, made by Roost Home Furnishings, also is available through Summer House.

The Tent

After calling around to top safari operations for leads, the couple ordered their extra-large, heavy-duty tent online from Exclusive Tents. Thanks to the mild Northern California weather, the tent is up year-round. Should there be a chill, a Batania Moroccan wool pom-pom blanket woven for L'Aviva Home keeps guests cozy. A Klein canvas and leather electrical bag from Guideboat Co. in Mill Valley stores provisions for visitors.

01 The Privy

No sleeping quarters, no matter how scenic, are complete without a convenient bathroom. This one—on a platform that matches the bedroom's—shares a corrugated steel roof with an open-air shower. Teak-stained knotty pine paneling, a stainless steel shower wall, and a poured-concrete floor can stand up to weather year-round.

02 Cleaning Supplies

A Murchison-Hume bathroom kit provides cleanup aid for both the shower and the showerers. Brushes from Gardenista-favorite Redecker are available in the States from Crate & Barrel.

03 Context Is Everything

A checked tray from Tokyo-based Fog Linen stylishly keeps a roll of toilet paper dry even if rain makes the floor wet.

SAN ANSELMO, CALIFORNIA

The Ultimate Chicken Coop

As Kathryn Freeman's yard proves, all it takes to turn a Marin County, California, edible garden into a small farm is a few chickens and an airy coop. With friendly offerings of fresh eggs every day, the neighbors don't complain.

OWNER

Kathryn Freeman

DESIGNER

Janell Denler Hobart, Denler Hobart Gardens

OPPOSITE: The walk-in chicken coop features a double set of slide bolt latches and two layers of welded mesh fencing. A photogenic assortment of laying hens (order a Murray McMurray Hatchery catalog to review the full range) hunt and peck safe from raccoons and hawks (and the feral cats that keep rodents under control).

The Long View

The sustainability-minded Freeman wanted a garden that required minimal water but worked hard for her family. Landscape designer Janell Hobart complied, putting in artificial turf to make a play space that withstands both constant use and chronic drought. A velvety border of boxwood backed by Osiana roses, 'Limelight' hydrangea (*Hydrangea paniculata*), and laurel encircles the yard. Beyond the coop, a forest of gigantic bamboo—"Their trunks are the size of soup cans," says Hobart—provides complete privacy.

Room to Roost

In most coops, collecting eggs requires some stooping. This shed-sized structure allows farmers the luxury of standing upright. Wood shavings, another civilized touch, keep the coop smelling sweet and make it easy to sweep out droppings. Just beyond the coop's fencing are the beginnings of a deliberate bramble that will eventually include raspberries, blackberries, and a climbing Eden rose.

01 Homemade

A full palette of farm-fresh eggs (the blue-hued eggs are from Araucana hens, made famous in the United States by farmer/blue-green lover Martha Stewart). Eggs last six months—but with each hen laying one a day, better to eat them right away.

02 Ready for Her Close-up

Speckled Sussex hens, like this one, lay light-brown eggs. The Sussex breed is one of several laying hens that can be used for meat as well. But most produce eggs throughout their lives (an average of eight years), so there's little temptation to consign them to the pot.

03 A Day's Work

The chickens were chosen for their looks as well as their output. A blue Polish hen regards her latest (the white one).

01

02

03

The Ultimate Chicken Coop

Annexing the Outdoors

A Courtyard Oasis for Entertaining

When San Francisco tastemaker Sam Hamilton turned her interiors business into a beautiful kitchen and culinary store in California, she also transformed a pocket courtyard into a chic outdoor lunchroom.

OWNER/DESIGNER

Sam Hamilton, March

OPPOSITE: The staff at March eats together outdoors nearly every day, "unless it's rainy (which seems to be never)," says Sam Hamilton. Her partner in kitchen design, Brian Espinoza (formerly of Chez Panisse), does the honors. The staff uses the same high-end European tableware that March sells—splatterware plates from Italy's Pugliese region, handblown crystal water pitcher and glasses by Lobmeyr in Hans Harald Rath's 1952 Alpha design, and European linen napkins hand cut and sewn in Ghent, New York, by Boxwood. Hamilton scoffs at those who worry about bringing their best pieces outdoors: "I don't see a problem with it at all, unless you don't have some substantial flat surfaces for folks to put things down on."

01 Concrete Flow

"The physical layout of the store, with the alley leading to the surprise of the garden and carriage house, felt reminiscent of spaces I'd experienced in the UK and Europe," says Hamilton, singling out Egg in London, Corso Como in Milan, and Merci in Paris. A nearly continuous concrete floor ties the main shop (where a working AGA stove lives) and the carriage house to the alley kitchen and garden lunchroom. Lemon trees in orangerie boxes ("They attract hummingbirds," says Hamilton) were the first residents of the mild-climate courtyard. The trees were joined by edible plants, herbs, and olive trees as March became a kitchen store.

02 Wabi-Sabi Kitchen

Wall hooks, a shelf, and a butcher-block countertop transform an outdoor sink into a kitted-out kitchen, stocked with basics including Blackcreek Mercantile and Trading Co. cutting boards, and Blackcreek's blade oil to keep the office collection of Wüsthof knives conditioned.

03 Versatility

With limited surfaces, double-duty pieces such as walnut live-edge boards (useful for chopping garlic as well as for serving) are critical. A mortar and pestle is another workhorse in the March kitchen.

04 Leafy Greens
Containers full of flat-leaf parsley and mixed lettuces in concrete planters line the courtyard and find themselves on the lunch menu daily.

05 Indoor-Outdoor Luxe
Stainless-steel Fantasia Sunflower flatware from northern Italy–based designer Mepra is made in a factory operated by the third generation of the same family; in the 1980s, the company expanded its line to include mixed-materials, heirloom-quality tableware. Sold in five-piece place settings, the flatware is also available in colors other than yellow, by special order.

06 Cool Spot
The refrigerator, inherited from an upstairs apartment, is tucked away in a corner shed, behind a door a few steps from the outdoor dining area.

Be Seated

Outfitting the open-air lunchroom are a woven rattan umbrella with a black granite base heavy enough to keep it upright in a tempest and a Belgian bluestone table, both from Sempre. Glass stools by Henry Dean of Antwerp take up the least amount of space while providing the maximum cachet and durability. Not-quite-black exterior paint provides a stylish backdrop; try Farrow & Ball's Off-Black or Benjamin Moore's Black Forest Green for a similar effect.

Design Ideas

When it comes to outdoor living and design, sometimes the smallest tweaks make the biggest difference: Replacing an eyesore of a mailbox with a sturdy, handsome, life-lasting classic; creating a washing station for sandy feet if you live by the beach; or planting a scented carpet of herbs for a perfumed patio. We've divided this chapter into three sections: The Ultimate DIY Work Space (ten easy projects that add up to one stylish workstation); Finishing Touches (fast fixes for an instant update); and Hardscaping Details (paths and drainage solutions).

The Ultimate DIY Work Space

We have a theory about work spaces (both indoor and
outdoor): the more pleasant and well organized they are,
the more motivated you'll be to tackle the task at hand.
In that spirit, we've come up with ten easy DIY projects for
creating the ultimate functional, beautiful garden workstation.
Do one project, or do them all—with our monochromatic
color palette, you'll end up with an instant outdoor room and
an elegant backdrop to greenery. Most of the materials are
available at your neighborhood hardware store or at
the nearest IKEA.

By Alexa Hotz

01

Dramatic Fence Backdrop

Painting an existing fence or exterior wall in a dark shade can create drama, improve the impact of your greenery, and instantly define a space.

What you need:

- Painter's canvas drop cloth (optional)
- Dark-gray exterior paint in an eggshell finish
  (we used Farrow & Ball's Railings, which is so dark it looks almost black)
- Paint roller and paintbrush
- Metal paint tray

STEP 1: Make sure the fence surface is clean and dry. If your existing fence is especially weather-beaten or lichen-covered, consider power washing it first.

STEP 2: Apply two generous coats of paint, allowing the first to dry completely before applying the second.

The Ultimate DIY Work Space

Design Ideas

02

Outdoor Worktable

Start with a pair of sawhorses or trestles and add an inexpensive tabletop. Bonus points: the worktable can become a serving table or bar when you entertain (see page 286).

What you need:

- Painter's canvas drop cloth (optional)
- 1 pair of wooden sawhorses or trestles (we used beech Finnvard trestles with shelves from IKEA)
- 1 wooden tabletop (we used a 47½-by-23⅝-inch birch tabletop from IKEA)
- Dark-gray exterior paint in an eggshell finish (we used Farrow & Ball's Railings)
- Paint roller and paintbrush
- Metal paint tray

STEP 1: Apply two coats of paint to the trestles and tabletop, allowing the first to dry completely before applying the second. (No need to sand or strip!)

STEP 2: Lay the tabletop across the trestles.

The Ultimate DIY Work Space

Design Ideas

03

Flowerpot Pendant Light

This project was inspired by the Australian eco-designer Joost Bakker, who's famous for using terra-cotta in surprising ways. You only need to add wiring to turn a simple terra-cotta pot into a garden-worthy light shade. We painted the cord yellow for added visual interest. Use a globe incandescent lightbulb to cast a soft, flattering light.

What you need:

- Painter's canvas drop cloth
- 1 can Rust-Oleum Painter's Touch 2x Sun Yellow exterior spray paint, high-gloss finish
- 1 cord set (consider the weatherproof Fantado Single Socket Pendant Light Commercial Grade Outdoor Cord Kit if you plan to use the fixture in an exposed outdoor area)
- Wire cutters
- One 4-inch terra-cotta pot
- Wire stripper
- One 15-amp quick wire plug
- 1 clear globe 40-watt incandescent lightbulb
- 1 ceiling hook
- Phillips-head screwdriver

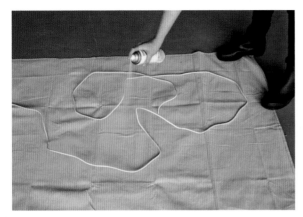

STEP 1: Cover a work surface in a well-ventilated room or outdoors with a drop cloth. Paint the cord with two coats of glossy yellow spray paint. Let dry.

STEP 2: Using wire cutters, snip the plug off the pendant cord. Thread the cord through the drainage hole in the bottom of the terra-cotta pot (the light-socket end must be *inside* the pot).

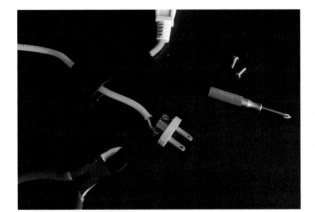

STEP 3: Use a wire stripper to strip off about a half inch of casing to expose the two wires on the cord's open end. Follow the installation instructions included with your plug to attach the wires to the plug. After assembling, screw in the lightbulb.

STEP 4: Suspend the pendant light from a hook in your porch ceiling or covered overhang.

The Ultimate DIY Work Space

Design Ideas

04

Dip-Dye Garden Tools

As William Morris said, "Have nothing in your house that you do not know to be useful, or believe to be beautiful." The same goes for your outdoor space—right down to your tools. Transform a generic, mismatched set of tools into display-worthy trophies by painting their handles and adding leather hanging straps. For an added sheen, we used high-gloss paint.

What you need:

- Painter's canvas drop cloth (optional)
- 1 shovel (ours is a Joseph Bentley stainless-steel model)
- 1 wood-handled garden fork
  (for one similar to ours, go to Burgon & Ball)
- Hand tools (Sophie Conran makes a hand fork and hand trowel similar to ours, available at Williams-Sonoma)
- Sandpaper (optional)
- Masking tape
- Dark-gray exterior paint in a high-gloss finish
  (we used Farrow & Ball's Railings)
- Paintbrush
- Black leather cord (available at Leather Cord USA)
- Scissors

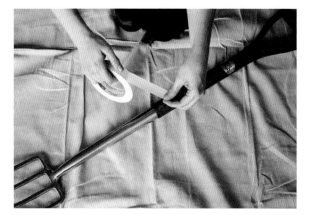

STEP 1: If any of your tool handles are varnished, sand the handles before painting. Cover the metal next to the handle of each tool with masking tape to avoid a mess.

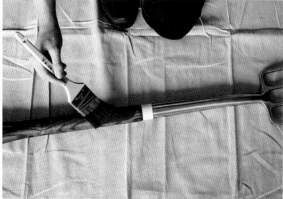

STEP 2: For long tools, give the handles two generous coats of paint with a paintbrush, allowing each coat to dry fully before applying the next.

STEP 3: For short tools, dip dye the handles by holding the metal end of each tool and slowly lowering its handle into the paint up to the desired point (mark it with a pencil if you want to be precise). Prop up the tools so the handles don't touch anything. After they dry, apply a second coat.

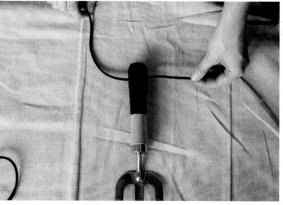

STEP 4: String a generous 24-inch length of cord through each short handle, make a loop, and tie off. Trim excess cord.

05

Organized Tool Storage

Work is more enjoyable when the tools you use are sturdy and beautiful and kept within easy reach. We added convenient storage options to our outdoor work space by adding hanging hooks and a wall-mounted shelf. A canvas bag is ideal for storing smaller tools and odds and ends.

What you need:

- Painter's canvas drop cloth (optional)
- 1 wall shelf (we used an Ekby Osten model from IKEA)
- 2 shelf brackets (we used an Ekby Stilig model from IKEA)
- Dark-gray exterior paint in a high-gloss finish (we used Farrow & Ball's Railings)
- Paintbrush
- Carpenter's level
- Tape measure
- Pencil
- 4 wood screws
- Power drill
- Four ⅞-inch nickel cup hooks
- 1 durable bag for smaller tools (ours is from Steele Canvas)

STEP 1: Paint the wall shelf and brackets, using two coats to cover surfaces evenly; allow to dry completely between coats.

STEP 2: Use a tape measure and carpenter's level to determine where you want to place the wood screws to hold up the brackets. Use a pencil to mark the screw placement.

STEP 3: Attach the brackets to the wall (or fence, as we did) with the wood screws.

STEP 4: Place the shelf on top of the brackets.

STEP 5: Screw cup hooks into the wall or fence to hang other tools.

STEP 6: Place smaller tools, gloves, et cetera, into a bag.

The Ultimate DIY Work Space

Design Ideas

06

Container Garden on Wheels

A portable planter on casters can be moved around in search of sunny outdoors spots, or migrate inside in cold weather. We painted our box pale gray to harmonize with the other elements in our outdoor room.

What you need:

- Painter's canvas drop cloth (optional)
- One 36-by-12-inch planter (ours is the cedar Window Box Planter from Chelsea Garden Center)
- Pale-gray exterior paint in a high-gloss finish (we used Farrow & Ball's Purbeck Stone)
- Paint roller and paintbrush
- Metal paint tray
- Power drill
- Four 3-inch steel swivel casters
- 16 wood screws
- River rocks
- 1 bag of potting soil
- Plants of your choice

STEP 1: Paint the exterior of the planter in two coats of high-gloss paint, allowing the first coat to dry fully before applying the next.

STEP 2: To attach the casters, first predrill four holes on each underside corner of the box for the wood screws, using a drill bit the same size as the screws. Attach the casters using wood screws. If the box doesn't already have drainage holes, drill a few.

STEP 3: Line the bottom of the box with river rocks for drainage; fill with potting soil.

STEP 4: Add plants and water well.

07

Painted Cinder-Block Planters

This tiered planter fits in a small space and is ideal for growing potted herbs or starter plants. It also serves as a surprisingly sophisticated sculptural element.

What you need:

- Painter's canvas drop cloth (optional)
- Three 16-by-8-by-8-inch two-cove cinder blocks
- Pale-gray exterior paint in a high-gloss finish
  (we used Farrow & Ball's Purbeck Stone)
- Paint roller and paintbrush
- Metal paint tray
- 3 steel 14-by-18-inch air vent grilles
- 1 tube DAP Kwik Seal Plus Kitchen and Bath Adhesive
- 2 yards of burlap fabric
- 1 or more bags of potting soil
- Plants of your choice (we planted sage, oregano, a fern, and a bonsai juniper tree)
- Plastic sheeting, cut to fit (optional)

STEP 1: Paint the outside of all three cinder blocks in high-gloss paint.

STEP 2: To prevent soil from leaking out the bottom of the blocks, attach air vent grilles: squeeze a generous line of adhesive caulk onto the underside of the grilles, making sure there's enough adhesive to contact the cement block when you flip it over. Wipe off excess caulk.

STEP 3: Place a grille on one open side of each cinder block, then turn the block over so its weight will help the caulk adhere while it dries. Allow the caulk to dry before potting.

STEP 4: To provide a base for the soil, cut the burlap into four 12-by-12-inch squares. Crumple them and tuck them into one hole of two blocks, and two holes of the third block.

STEP 5: Add soil on top of the burlap. Fill halfway so you can position plants at the correct depth. Remove the plants from their plastic pots and tuck them into the soil, then add more soil to fill the cinder block.

STEP 6: Now stack the three blocks: the two with the single plants are your base; the block with two plants sits on top. Note: If you plan to put the planters on a wooden surface, line the surface first with a sheet of cut-to-fit heavy plastic.

08

Ornamental Cabbage Kokedama

Inspired by Japanese *kokedama*, a traditional art form whose name translates as "moss ball," we turned a hardy ornamental cabbage into an attractive houseplant. The result is a low-maintenance plant that doesn't even need a pot to survive.

What you need:

- Mixing bowl
- 1 package all-purpose bonsai tree soil
  (*akadama*; find it online or at a specialty bonsai store)
- 1 package peat moss
- Small potted ornamental cabbage
  (from a local garden center or Home Depot)
- 1 package sphagnum moss
- Cotton twine
- 1 package natural green sheet moss (optional)
- Scissors or garden clippers
- Heavy-duty twine (we used Nutscene jute twine)

STEP 1: Fill the bowl with a roughly 7:3 mix of peat moss to bonsai soil. Add water and mix with your hands. Continue adding water until the soil holds together.

STEP 2: Form the soil into a ball 4 to 5 inches in diameter.

STEP 3: Remove the cabbage from its plastic pot and gently pull away excess soil from the roots. Using two fingers, make a deep indentation in the soil ball. Tuck the plant's roots into the hole, adding more soil as needed.

STEP 4: Moisten the sphagnum moss and place a layer of it on the table. Put the soil ball and plant on top of it, and wrap in the sphagnum moss to cover the soil.

STEP 5: Wrap the moss-covered ball with cotton twine, adding sheet moss along the way, if desired.

STEP 6: Wrap the ball a second time with heavier twine and tie off, leaving enough twine to hang the plant, if desired. Hang the *kokedama* from a shaded shelf (moss loves shade), or rest it in a bowl with a thin layer of water. Spray daily to keep the moss well moistened.

09

Windproof Outdoor Tablecloth

For an outdoor tablecloth, we like to use an inexpensive canvas drop cloth for both looks and longevity. These simple C-clamps are strong enough to hold the cloth in place on a breezy day.

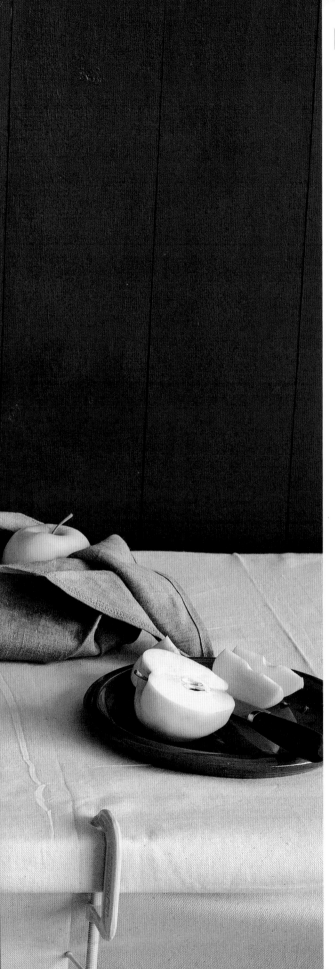

What you need:

- 2 painter's canvas drop cloths, one for painting and one for covering the table
- 4 small adjustable C-clamps (check that they open wide enough to fit your tabletop)
- 1 can Rust-Oleum Painter's Touch 2x Sun Yellow exterior spray paint, high-gloss finish

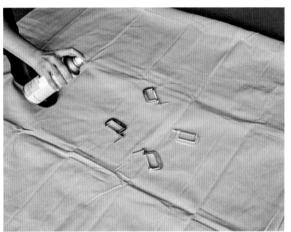

STEP 1: Set the C-clamps on a covered surface in a well-ventilated room or outdoors; spray on the paint. Allow to dry. Give the clamps a second coat, so the metal is well covered.

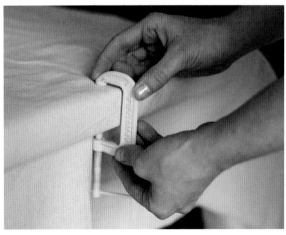

STEP 2: Lay the cloth on the table and screw on the four clamps to hold the cloth in place.

10

Simple Outdoor Sink

An outdoor sink makes cleaning up after a gardening project infinitely easier. It's also handy for washing just-picked vegetables and herbs. You can build this project around an existing outdoor tap, or hire a plumber to install an outdoor faucet. We chose a faucet that can be used as a tap and also as the screw-in base for a garden hose. For the sink, a simple bucket will do. Wash up using biodegradable soap, and you can use the water in your garden.

What you need:

- 1 faucet (we used a Chicago Faucets Inside Sill Fitting Faucet, Model 293-369COLDCP, with lever handle)

- One 10-liter galvanized bucket (we used one with a wooden handle from Labour and Wait)

- 1 birch Pan & Vegetable Brush by Iris Hantverk, for cleaning garden produce

The Big Picture

The ten projects add up to one DIY workspace.

Finishing Touches

Embrace the one-off with these inspired solutions for solving a design problem or creating a moment of beauty in an outdoor space (where even drainage can be stylish). Here, a few examples of nice-to-have extras and hardscape ideas that give a garden personality and purpose.

01

Mismatched Chairs

A trio of butterfly chairs (for sources, see the "Gardenista 100" chapter) is all it takes to make an outdoor living room. Pea gravel, pavers, and edging rocks of bluestone keep the palette consistent, receding into the background to frame the furniture. Playing against the clean, rounded shapes of the chairs, dense foliage (including monstera, *Grevillea robusta*, and ferns) defines the perimeter.

02

Dent-Proof Mailbox

An indestructible mailbox by Veeders Mailboxes of Ohio has the familiar bread-loaf shape and proportions of its flimsier sheet metal cousins but is built of welded steel. It will withstand the efforts of vandals with baseball bats and acts of God alike; branches may crash down in a storm but will not mar its iconic silhouette.

03

Dog-Washing Station

To make a simple dog-washing station, install a hand shower on a garage wall (shown here above a wooden platform designed for drainage). For a similar wand-style fixture with a cross handle, consider the Modo Tubular Hand Shower in an oil-rubbed bronze finish, available at Signature Hardware.

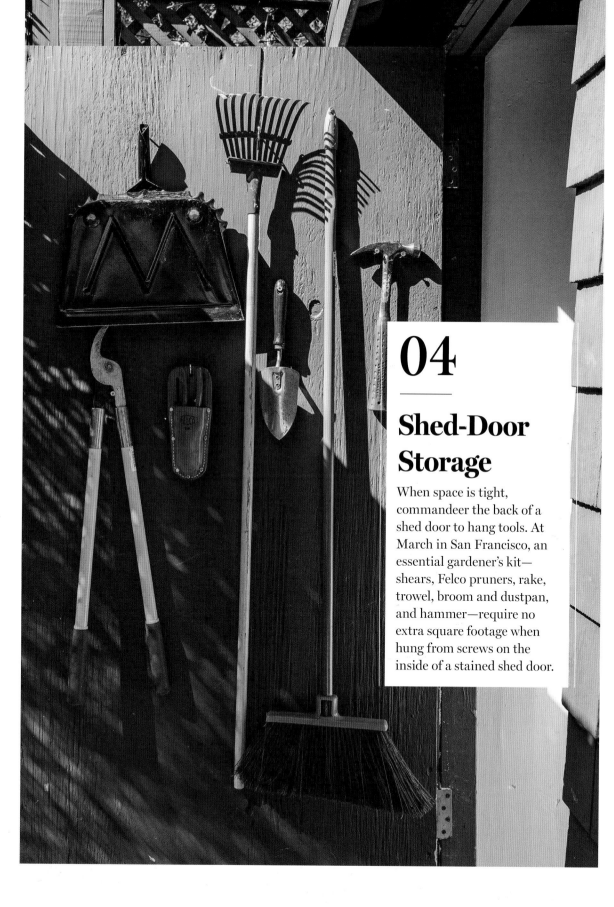

04

Shed-Door Storage

When space is tight, commandeer the back of a shed door to hang tools. At March in San Francisco, an essential gardener's kit—shears, Felco pruners, rake, trowel, broom and dustpan, and hammer—require no extra square footage when hung from screws on the inside of a stained shed door.

05

All-Season Kitchenette

This food-prep station has a roof for shade and shelter, borrowing a design idea from covered porches. A stone-slab countertop and sink are rugged as well as stylish, and the gooseneck faucet, fashioned from standard plumbing parts, resists rust and corrosion—no protective cover is necessary to survive the winter.

06

Weatherproof Faucet

Attached to copper plumbing pipes is a heavy-duty faucet from PurePro, whose line of plumbing products is sold only to contractors through distributor F. W. Webb. The sixteen-point red wheel handles are standard, and can be found at local hardware stores.

07

Foot Shower

From the seashore, a staircase ascends a cliff to the garden, where beachgoers stop upon their return to rinse away sand in a galvanized bucket. Mounted to a wood post is a commercial-grade faucet and a red wheel handle (Amazon sells a similar model from Larsen Supply Co., a maker of plumbing parts). Water in the bucket sees subsequent use in the garden, where it can be used to water potted plants.

08

Irrigation System

A pitchfork leaning against a 4-foot-high chicken wire fence has a handle at just the right height to prop up a hose for an impromptu sprinkler, directing water precisely to where it's most needed.

09

The Reel Thing

After an old oak tree came down in a Cape Cod garden, a wishbone branch found new life as a hose reel that (unlike its plastic counterparts) disappears into the garden. Get the look by using a posthole digger to bury a found branch 3 feet deep.

10

Clean Living

An outdoor laundry shed at a Cape Cod summerhouse takes up less than 15 square feet of space and has the perfect dimensions to hold a stacked washer and dryer.

11

Simplest Shower

In a private corner of her garden, Christine Ten Eyck sited an outdoor shower enclosure framed with the same wire mesh as her garden gate. Her husband, Gary Deaver, who installed the exposed copper plumbing, covered a plastic shower head with an old tomato can and reused a metal soap dish from the house. Water drains directly into the garden soil.

Hardscaping Details

In an outdoor space, sometimes the most important design elements are those that no one notices. And while it's true that the hardscape plays a supporting role, to give a garden good bones, you should pay special attention to the design of structural elements such as paths and drains.

Paths

Often the destination doesn't matter as much as the journey. That's as true in the garden as it is in life. Here are a few beautifully designed paths—laid with materials ranging from gravel to pine needles—that make us realize we don't need to be anywhere else.

01

Triumphal Arch

A privet archway points visitors toward a garden path. A carpet of straw inhibits weeds, aids drainage, and slowly turns to mulch from foot traffic. In John Derian's Cape Cod garden, landscape designer Tim Callis transplanted two mature privets, cut down to 3-foot nubs before they were moved, to flank a garden gate. Expect privet to grow as much as 3 feet in one year.

02

Making Tracks

A grass path shaded by trees and mown regularly in summer months feels good under bare feet and causes no disruption to the surrounding natural landscape.

03

Woodland Walkway

Bordered by beds of *Nepeta* (catmint) and *Oenothora* (evening primrose), a pine needle walkway feels soft underfoot. To create a similar permeable path from scratch, dig an 8-inch-deep walkway and fill with a 5-inch base layer of gravel. With a rake, add a 3-inch layer of pine needles, which will decompose over the course of several months. Once a year, add a fresh layer of pine needles.

04

Walk the Planks

The same wood rafters that builders typically use for framing can create a rustic plank walkway with a low price tag and high style. You can plant wildflowers in the grass alongside, as garden designer Tim Callis did in this Cape Cod garden. "A wild lawn reminds me of my grandmother's fantastic backyard," he says. He plants clover and violets in the turf because "the world doesn't have enough violets."

05

Mixed Media

Irregular bluestone pavers—pieces of stone with natural, uneven shapes—can be set in a bed of "Mexican Mix" pea gravel. (Individual pieces of pea gravel typically range from ⅜ to ⅝ inch in diameter.) Shades of gray blend together and complement the blue tones of surrounding succulents on a Los Angeles entryway path designed by landscape designer Judy Kameon.

06

A Clipped Greeting

A winding path of bluestone pea gravel relies on a bordering boxwood hedge (clipped low and tight) to set a formal tone in Janell Denler Hobart's garden in Ross, California. Edging strips extend an inch higher than the path to prevent gravel from migrating into the garden beds.

07

Welcome to the Jungle

A gravel path looks untamed, tropical, and mysterious because plants like ferns and succulents are encouraged to encroach. To save water, micro-precision spray heads direct the flow to plants' roots.

Drainage Solutions

Drainage is one of those issues everyone has to deal with but few talk about. Elevate this hardscape element from boring to brilliant with simple designs that recognize how lucky we are to have water at all.

01

Low Profile

A permeable layer of fine gray gravel (that matches the color of adjacent concrete pavers) prevents rainwater from puddling in the small, enclosed space, instead filtering it into an underground French drain that runs alongside the building's foundation in the garden courtyard behind Sam Hamilton's store, March, in San Francisco.

02

Visible Improvement

Set into a bluestone paver angled to funnel water underground, a round metal drain grate connects to a drywell beneath a Brooklyn garden. A small platform to display potted plants turns this hardscape element into a design vignette.

03

Unified Palette

Foundation drainage around the perimeter of Molly and Eric Glasgow's barn at their organic farm on Martha's Vineyard has a layer of large, smooth rocks edged by stone posts to separate the French drain system from an adjacent path of pea gravel. Although different in size and shape, all the stones used in the hardscape design belong to the same red color family, creating a pleasing design element.

04

Gutter Talk

Instead of mounted gutters on the facade, a Cape Cod house
has a French drain wide enough to capture rainwater from
the roof's drip line.

05

Living Gutter-Free

Lending support to a permeable concrete terrace, perimeter drains set into a trench of quarter-inch crushed gravel handle extra rainwater at the Kinderhook, New York, weekend home of architect Steven Harris and landscape designer Lucien Rees Roberts.

06

Raise the Roof

Water runs off a lawn of artificial grass (edged with strips of ipe wood) and into a drainage trough through a layer of smooth, rounded stones on garden designer Julie Farris's Brooklyn rooftop.

The Gardenista 100

A roundup of our all-time favorite everyday objects: from digging tools to outdoor dining tables, these classic essentials are as pleasurable to collect as they are practical to use.

With nutshell histories by Kendra Wilson
of Ancient Industries

01 Variopinte Enameled Cutlery

Capable of elevating a picnic to banquet status, Variopinte's dishwasher-friendly line of enameled tableware is hand-stamped with Italian designer Stefania di Petrillo's signature. The outdoor cutlery pieces—including a knife, fork, spoon, and dessert spoon—are elegant enough to find a home indoors as well as out.

WHY IT WORKS: Retro picnic ware with modern lines
WHERE TO GET IT: variopinte.com

02 Audubon Field Guide Series

When you own a complete sixteen-volume set of these definitive field guides from the venerable wildlife conservation group, you can tailor your walks to different aspects of the natural world, whether it's a rocks-and-minerals hike or an insects-and-spiders investigation. Tuck a guide in your pocket to make any outing on foot immanently more interesting, particularly for the reluctant hiker. Good color photographs make IDs easy.

WHY IT WORKS: Vinyl-covered wisdom gleaned from two centuries of bird-watchers
WHERE TO GET IT: bestmadeco.com

03 All Heal Salve

A gardener's secret weapon, this salve from Toronto-based herbalist Denise Williams soothes cracked and chapped skin with all-natural ingredients you might find in your own garden. Rose-thorn pricks and garden scratches don't stand a chance against her formulation, a healing concoction of flowers, herbs, and essential oils (including comfrey, burdock, plantain leaf, chamomile, and lavender).

WHY IT WORKS: Common comfrey's medicinal powers, in a compact container
WHERE TO GET IT: mattercompany.com

04 French Florists' Bucket

Florists prize vintage metal-topped tables; even a well-worn one will withstand puddles, prickles, and soggy piles. For those of us who lack a designated flower room, the florists' bucket offers the same benefits. What's more, you can carry it around the garden (like an unbreakable vase) as you cut stems. The cool cylindrical interior is so perfect for conditioning flowers, they may never make the leap into a smarter vase.

WHY IT WORKS: Garden to table; lighter than galvanized steel
WHERE TO GET IT: gardentrading.co.uk

05 Biergarten Table

Undoubtedly efficient for outdoor drinking, this beer garden table set shouldn't be limited to brewfests. Made in Germany, with a stain-resistant lacquer finish, the narrow 7-foot-long table and its two benches are easily brought out of storage and unfolded to feed a crowd. Push two tables together for even more surface space. These pieces are so good-looking they deserve to be kept out all the time, whether in the garden or in a space-constrained kitchen.

WHY IT WORKS: Foldaway furniture that doesn't need to be kept hidden
WHERE TO GET IT: oktoberfesthaus.com

06 Bonsai Scissors

Many centuries before the Shakers and the modernists, Japanese craftsmen did their bit for functional minimalism. Although they cannot claim to have invented the cross-blade scissor (the Romans got there first), they did develop this fluid shape, which accommodates an entire hand rather than just a forefinger and thumb. The scissors are associated with the trimming of bonsai trees, but their short, sharp blade makes them indispensable in the garden and around the house as well. They've been made on the island of Tanegashima for nine hundred years.

WHY THEY WORK: Twelfth-century ergonomics
WHERE TO GET THEM: bonsaioutlet.com, tortoisegeneralstore.com

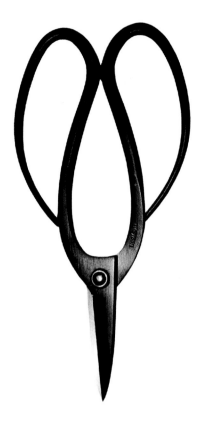

07 Meriwether Canvas Tent

For camping enthusiasts, the conical bell tent is a sturdy ally in the wilderness. Its thick canvas walls withstand water and wind, while the size and shape make it pleasant to inhabit. All these were practical considerations for brigadier general Henry Hopkins Sibley, who borrowed the concept from Native Americans in the 1850s. Sibley patented his invention in 1856, and soon after, the British Army took his tent, ensuring its success. It continues to be the preferred tent for lovers of the outdoors around the world.

WHY IT WORKS: Handsome accommodations for even the most unwilling camper
WHERE TO GET IT: shelter-co.com

08 Anti-fly Glass Sphere

Instead of trapping or zapping houseflies, use this glass sphere to persuade them to go elsewhere. Suspending a water-filled plastic bag has long been a folk remedy for keeping flies away from a market or a farmhouse back door. Mexican designer José de la O has taken the concept a step further by adding design rationale. His sphere is made of tough borosilicate glass; fill it with water and hang it by its leather rope. The glass creates refractions between sun and water to play havoc with the compound eyes of the poor flies, inducing them to buzz off.

WHY IT WORKS: Elegant pest solution
WHERE TO GET IT: kaufmann-mercantile.com

09 Willow Cloche

As the ground warms up in spring, tiny seedlings are vulnerable to late frost, wind, and passing animals. A woven willow cloche placed over a young plant discourages marauding creatures, giving even a pigeon pause, and it will remind you not to weed it out. To extend the life of willow, bring it indoors in winter. A small cloche can also serve as a ready-made framework for forced bulbs, whose foliage tends to flop over in comfortable temperatures.

WHY IT WORKS: Rustic utility
WHERE TO GET IT: williams-sonoma.com

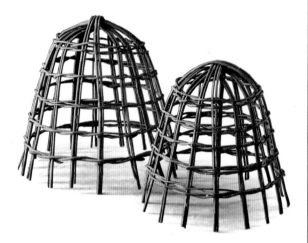

10 Best Measuring Tape

In some cases, it's not boasting to say you're the best. This solid, German-made tape measure is 10 meters (32½ feet) long and comes in a weatherproof, coated-steel case that evokes a well-balanced discus. The tape is heavy enough to lie flat where you place it; lay out a walkway, a garden bed, or a row of beans at your leisure. Then it retracts on a wish (with the help of a winding arm).

WHY IT WORKS: Last-a-lifetime quality to tuck into a tool bag
WHERE TO GET IT: guideboat.com

11 Cast-Iron Fire Bowl

The fire bowl signifies a gathering, a celebration with warmth. This model, designed by Søren Slebo, mimics the traditional welcoming style used on land as beacons to Danish ships at sea. A conical grate in the upper part of the bowl focuses the heat in the center for efficient burning while the ash collects in the base. Built-in handles ease transportation to the beach (its spiritual home); a stainless-steel grill may be added for those who feel that no outdoor fire is complete without cooking.

WHY IT WORKS: Minimalist Viking
WHERE TO GET IT: dwr.com

12 Fermob Classic Bistro Furniture

French bistro furniture is undeniably chic, but it was actually designed for efficiency: the foldaway tables and chairs were developed for street sellers and café owners who needed to pack up in a hurry. The original bistro chair was patented in 1889, the same year as the unveiling of the Eiffel Tower. Fermob, the caretaker of this iconic furniture, continues to finesse its durability as well as its joie de vivre, in a rainbow of colors that range from primary to rich and dark.

WHY IT WORKS: Fits in anywhere
WHERE TO GET IT: frenchbistrofurniture.com

13 Peterboro Bike Basket

For some, a cheery bike basket made of woven wood is reason enough to own a bicycle—nylon panniers belong to the world of goggles and Lycra. An Appalachian white ash basket perched on the handlebars may not be aerodynamic, but cycling is not always a sport. Pedaling at your own pace to the general store or farmers' market is a different kind of leisure. The Peterboro company has been weaving bike baskets in New Hampshire since 1854.

WHY IT WORKS: Symbol of the weekend
WHERE TO GET IT: kaufmann-mercantile.com

14 French Outdoor Thermometer

For the truth about the weather, check the thermometer by the back door. More personable than an app and less grandiose than a barometer, this simple enamel-coated device has remained unchanged for at least a century. Hang this in a sheltered spot.

WHY IT WORKS: Tells it like it is
WHERE TO GET IT: labourandwait.co.uk

15 Swedish Potting Table

Create an instant potting shed with a 30-inch-wide potting table small enough to tuck into a corner of nearly any room. From Scandinavia, where gardeners set great store by their flowering houseplants, this pine potting table (made of Forest Stewardship Council–certified wood) has a florist-approved, waterproof zinc tabletop; three drawers for storing shears and a trowel; and a lower shelf where you can stack pots and planters when not in use.

WHY IT WORKS: As stylish as a dressing table
WHERE TO GET IT: gardenhome.se

16 Pothos Houseplant

Allow us to introduce *Scindapsus aures*. Or perhaps you two have already met? Known for its hardy resilience, pothos is a popular native of Southeast Asia that has made the transition to other climes gracefully enough to deserve a spot among the houseplants on most any windowsill. With waxy, heart-shaped leaves and an easygoing personality (it thrives in sun or shade, and needs water no more than once a week), pothos is the perfect pet, even for those with black thumbs.

WHY IT WORKS: Turns a black thumb green
WHERE TO GET IT: thesill.com (seasonally) or your local nursery

17 Tablecloth Clamps

A set of four weatherproof clamps will ensure an elegant outdoor dining experience on even the windiest day. Manufactured by Germany-based GEFU-Küchenboss (maker of the first food mill in 1943), the stainless-steel clips can be adjusted to grip tabletops of almost any thickness. Known for engineering products to precise specifications, the company has designed the clips with slightly rounded edges to avoid nicking any stray elbows that might be resting on the edge of a picnic table.

WHY THEY WORK: Removes weather worries
WHERE TO GET THEM: manufactum.com

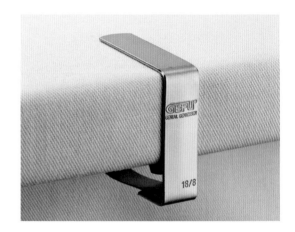

18 Redecker Flowerpot Brush

Nobody manufactures more specialty brushes—anyone need a mushroom brush, by the way?—than Germany-based Redecker (in the business of bristles since 1935). The handmade flowerpot brush is a precise tool and a thing of beauty, with natural fiber bristles and a sturdy wooden handle made of oiled beech. The bristles' graduated diameter increases the efficiency with which a gardener can remove soil and accumulated debris from the bottom and sides of a plant pot.

WHY IT WORKS: The right tool for the job
WHERE TO GET IT: housekeepingstore.co.uk

19 Shaker Broom

Just as the Shakers displayed their brooms, so should we. This is particularly true when they are made in the United States of natural broom corn (a type of grass grown for this purpose). Haydenville Broomworks continues the tradition in the Berkshires of Massachusetts, making the handles from coppiced sassafras (strong and lightweight), attaching the broom corn with eight-gauge wire, and using a restored nineteenth-century vise to flatten the broom as it's stitched (for a wider sweep). The Shaker broom remains a symbol of honest living—just the thing for tidying the back steps.

WHY IT WORKS: Value-added virtue for serious sweepers
WHERE TO GET IT: haydenvillebroomworks.com

20 Haws Plant Mister

This metal plant mister is made in England by Haws, known for high-quality watering cans since 1886 (when company founder John Haws began selling a perfectly balanced design that was easy for gardeners to carry and to tip). The old-world pump action increases the pleasure of nurturing orchids and other fine houseplants, and the mister is stylish enough to display beside its leafy charges, instead of being banished to the cupboard.

WHY IT WORKS: Small and affordable, yet hints at the grandest hothouse
WHERE TO GET IT: shopterrain.com

21 Versailles Planter

In the seventeenth century, royal gardener André Le Nôtre cleverly conceived of a container to allow the citrus trees at Versailles to move in and out of the Orangerie with the seasons. A modernist version has even simpler lines, because it is a truth universally acknowledged that garden plants need no additional adornment. Made of strips of grained oak, the planter has an unsealed surface so water can drain through cracks between the planks. A square Reclaimed French Oak Staccato version is available in four graduated sizes (plus a trough version).

WHY IT WORKS: A classically serene backdrop to greenery
WHERE TO GET IT: restorationhardware.com

22 Whichford Terra-Cotta Pot

Although classic terra-cotta has long been a mainstay of the English country house garden, the Cotswolds pot maker Whichford is relatively new on the scene. The pottery was started in 1976 as a family business and is still run by its founder, Jim Keeling, who has a degree in archaeology and history from Cambridge. The company name has become synonymous with iconic shapes and designs that are easily identified even before the logo reveals itself. Some of the most notable gardens in the Cotswolds are neighbors to the pottery, displaying Whichford pots to best effect.

WHY IT WORKS: Robust and frostproof, with unerring design
WHERE TO GET IT: whichfordpottery.com

23 Steele Canvas Tote Bag

These hard-working tote bags come in wide, tall, medium, and small sizes—and the many choices reflect both their popularity and their usefulness to the gardener. Manufacturer Steele Canvas has been cutting cloth since 1921, when the Cambridge, Massachusetts, company began supplying the coal industry with durable carryalls. The classic tote has reinforced handles and a boxed bottom, and it stands upright and open while you fill it. We've found the company lives up to its promise: "Our tote bags will hold your heaviest bundles without tearing."

WHY IT WORKS: Stylish strongman
WHERE TO GET IT: steelecanvas.com

24 Sussex Trug

The body of a genuine Sussex trug is made from shaved willow boards, normally reserved for cricket bats; its rim and handle are of sweet chestnut. The word *trug* derives from the Anglo-Saxon, referring to a boat-shaped scoop used to measure grain. After Queen Victoria took a liking to some trugs shown at the Great Exhibition of 1851, they became domestic favorites for carrying flowers, vegetables, or sewing supplies. The round trug has such a pleasing shape that it may never make it outdoors at all.

WHY IT WORKS: Remarkably lightweight and durable
WHERE TO GET IT: thetrugstore.co.uk

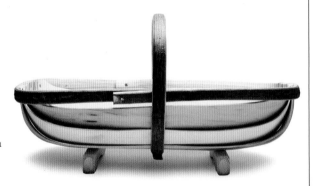

25 Dash & Albert Striped Outdoor Rug

It was the English who had the idea of the "outdoor room" to protect us from the wilderness beyond the garden gate. They enclosed a space with tall hedges and let it go at that. Here's an improvement: an outdoor rug to define the room (and offer hints about where to place the sofa and chairs). Dash & Albert's handsome rugs look just as good in an indoor setting, but why waste their weather-resistant qualities?

WHY IT WORKS: Comforts of home, outdoors
WHERE TO GET IT: dashandalbert.annieselke.com

26 Outdoor Bench

With a background in design (having cofounded *Wallpaper* magazine), Paul de Zwart had a good idea of the bench he wanted when he was working on his new house in Dorset, but he couldn't find it. Hence the furniture design company Another Country was born in 2010. (In 2013, Another Country opened a showroom and shop in London's Marylebone.) This 63-inch outdoor bench, an archetypal shape, is solid oak with brass fittings and is protected with a wood oil finish. The company promises that it will "age gracefully like a yacht's deck."

WHY IT WORKS: A classic with improvements
WHERE TO GET IT: anothercountry.com

27 Brommö Chaise

Made of acacia wood and rope, IKEA's very reasonably priced modernist lounge chair has achieved icon status. We've sat on the comfortable, generously sized seat in gardens all over the world and can report that the design embodies the best chameleon qualities of classic, clean Scandinavian style (the chair looks good against any backdrop, from bare-bones to opulent). The happy price tag makes it possible to use this foldable, easily stored chair in an indoor setting—or to expose it to outdoor weather without guilt.

WHY IT WORKS: Matches everything you own
WHERE TO GET IT: ikea.com

28 Odlingsvitrin Miniature Greenhouse

From Scandinavian gardening supply company Kekkilä, the Odlingsvitrin portable greenhouse (which the company translates as "Green Vitrine") is made of Finnish pine. The compact greenhouse does not betray its flat-pack roots: the glass is real and the galvanized shelving is adjustable, with a fully functioning storage drawer at the base. A ventilation flap in the roof opens and closes automatically in reaction to the temperature within, maintaining the best environment for precious seedlings or orchids.

WHY IT WORKS: Glasshouse for a balcony
WHERE TO GET IT: manufactum.co.uk

29 Munstead Flower Glasses

A sensible woman, the renowned English garden designer Gertrude Jekyll knew that cut flowers are displayed to best effect in simple glass vessels. She had her vases handblown to her own specifications, wider at the top than at the bottom, with a sturdy base, and at heights designed for different types of stems: taller for roses, stouter for tulips. Fortunately, her flower glasses have recently been brought back into production by Jekyll's great-great-niece Christina Freyberg.

WHY THEY WORK: A meeting of craft and horticulture
WHERE TO GET THEM: gertrudejekylldesigns.com

30 Sun Valley Bronze Gate Latch

The familiar clack of a gate latch, like the bang of a screen door, signifies enjoyment of indoor-outdoor life. We shouldn't need to stop and give a gate latch our full attention. The impression, in the blur of the moment, should be of something geometrical and reassuringly solid. Hardware manufacturer Sun Valley Bronze's founder, Robert Commons, began casting his own in 1992 to meet the criteria. Nearly twenty-five years later the family-owned business relies on art-grade bronze to make reliable, top-quality castings.

WHY IT WORKS: The latch makes the gate
WHERE TO GET IT: sunvalleybronze.com

31 Haws Watering Can

Bringing to mind Beatrix Potter's Mr. McGregor, this watering can is proof that the Victorians were capable of designing household objects without flourish. John Haws was interested only in functionality, and in 1886 he came up with a watering can that was all about balance and ease of pouring. In so doing, he inadvertently created an object of beauty—oft copied— that has not been altered to this day.

WHY IT WORKS: Well-balanced and beautiful
WHERE TO GET IT: hawswateringcans.com

32 The Original Tree Swing

Whether hung from a branch or the sturdy beam of an outbuilding, a classic wooden swing says good things about those who have one. It will win you young friends and show everyone else that you know when to take a break. All you need are two lengths of sturdy rope, a 2-foot-long polished plank, and a spot to suspend it.

WHY IT WORKS: Prohibits use of electronic devices, as two hands are required for proper swinging
WHERE TO GET IT: theoriginaltreeswing.com

33 Dover Parkersburg Galvanized Tub

Based in West Virginia, Dover Parkersburg has been making utilitarian products since 1833, including a wide range of buckets, cans, and tubs for use in the garden or on the farm. What sets these humble vessels apart is that they are made of steel that has been hot-dipped in molten zinc to effectively resist corrosion. The galvanizing process results in a bright prismatic shine that softens to matte as it ages. The 15-inch-wide, 2¼-gallon tub multitasks: as a planter, an ice bucket, or a storage container.

WHY IT WORKS: Rustproof steel for outdoor use
WHERE TO GET IT: greatplainshardware.com

34 Trook

Firewood is not the only fate for a beloved tree felled by freak weather. Designer Geoffrey Fisher began to make hooks from branches after his lilac died from a cold winter in Buckinghamshire, England. The name is an amalgam of *tree* and *hook*, and each trook is unique. In fact, every one comes with an ID card to explain its provenance: not just the type of tree it was made from, but where the tree grew. Hang several in a mudroom or children's room—or put them outside in a sheltered area.

WHY IT WORKS: No trees were harmed in the making of this product
WHERE TO GET IT: geoffreyfisher.com, floragrubb.com

35 English Oak Doorstop

The Forest Stewardship Council, or FSC, is an international nonprofit founded in 1992 by a band of rogue businessmen and environmentalists concerned about responsible management of the world's forests. These FSC-certified oak doorstops might once have stood in an ancient grove, but one can sleep at night knowing that the forest has not since been flattened. The cunning, cheese-shaped wedge slides discreetly under a variety of door heights, proving very handy in sudden gusts of wind.

WHY IT WORKS: Conscientious objector to plastic
WHERE TO GET IT: ancientindustries.com

36 Flowering Spring Bulbs

Planting bulbs that naturalize is an effective and simple approach to gardening. Some advance planning is all that's needed. In autumn, take a collection of spring bulbs—narcissi, hyacinths, tulips, and muscari—and toss them over your shoulder with gay abandon. Then plant them just where they land, for a "naturalistic" look (at an appropriate depth for each type). Tulip bulbs prone to naturalizing, such as species tulips, can be planted and forgotten: just place them extra deep.

WHY THEY WORK: The little spring shoots say it all
WHERE TO GET THEM: whiteflowerfarm.com

37 Butterfly Chair

Popularly associated with midcentury modernist lounging, the butterfly began life as a wood-framed folding chair during the Crimean and Boer wars (it was patented by the British in 1877). Fifty years later, three Argentine architects replaced the wood with a single length of steel and exhibited the chair at a furniture fair in Buenos Aires. It caught the eye of MoMA's industrial design curator, Edgar Kaufmann Jr., who bought one for the museum and one for his parents' new country house, Fallingwater (designed by Frank Lloyd Wright). After Knoll acquired the U.S. production rights in 1947, about 5 million chairs were sold before the end of the 1950s. Today Circa50 in Vermont faithfully reproduces the chair.

WHY IT WORKS: Casual, affordable, looks good anywhere
WHERE TO GET IT: steelecanvas.com, circa50.com

38 Beeswax Tea Lights

Not to be wasted on jack-o'-lanterns, these candles from Chicago Honey Co-op offer an instant waft of natural luxury. They should be burned in an open holder, as they really do smell of freshly harvested honey. Elegantly hand-dipped beeswax tapers are all very well, but they tend to be saved for special occasions—this well-priced diffusion line can be lit up whenever a mood shift is required. Store in a cool, dark place.

WHY THEY WORK: Burn longer and with a better scent than ordinary wax candles
WHERE TO GET THEM: rodales.com

39 Ben Wolff Black Clay Pot

Wolff trained at the wheel of his father, master potter Guy Wolff. Father and son were both based in Litchfield County, a region of Connecticut packed with artists, so it's no surprise that Guy's circle has included the artist Alexander Calder and the architect Marcel Breuer. Ben Wolff excels in shapes fashioned from black or white clay; for him, terra-cotta takes a backseat.

WHY IT WORKS: Well-priced, traditional shape in monochrome shades
WHERE TO GET IT: benwolffpottery.com

40 Canyon Lantern

With a design that pays homage to American railroad lanterns of an earlier era, the rechargeable LED Canyon Lantern has a decidedly modern and eco-friendly outlook. In 2010, company founder Robert Workman created Barebones (currently based in Bluffdale, Utah) to lure more people into the garden—and beyond—with a range of thoughtfully designed tools and equipment. The lantern can charge your cell phone via USB port; the battery will last for four hours on its highest setting. A retractable lens allows you to adjust the beam of light to an ambient glow.

WHY IT WORKS: Keeps you Instagram-enabled in the woods
WHERE TO GET IT: guideboat.com

41 Sun Valley Bronze Doorknocker

Cabinetmaker Robert Commons felt compelled to start casting his own bronze door hardware in the early 1990s, after realizing that products currently available on the market lacked detail. Now his family-run business in Sun Valley, Idaho, provides something a little personal through every stage of manufacture and installation. After all, every front door is different (or so we would hope).

WHY IT WORKS: Traditional detail and technical know-how in Idaho
WHERE TO GET IT: sunvalleybronze.com

42 Variopinte Enamelware Picnic Plates

Moving away from its traditional image of campsite frugality, enamelware is making an unapologetic appearance on proper dining tables, indoors and out. Reimagined by Italians, Variopinte handmade enamel plates are consequently chic and vibrant. A simple translation of *variopinte* is "multicolored," yet these have plenty of white to calm things down. A stamped circle within each decarbonized steel plate recalls the familiar form of tin cans.

WHY THEY WORK: Unbreakable beauty, very stackable
WHERE TO GET THEM: variopinte.com

43 Fiddle-Leaf Fig Tree

To understand why a finicky native of West African lowland rain forests became the "it" houseplant of the past decade, one need look no further than *Ficus lyrata*'s moon-pie leaves. With their waxy roundness, the leaves complement all styles of interior design and add a much-needed reminder of the outdoors to indoor landscapes. Allow soil to dry out before watering (perform a fingertip test to make sure there's no moisture to a depth of 1 inch) and place it in indirect light. If you move it outdoors in warm weather, your tree will feel grateful for the air circulation—and reward you by growing to a maximum height of 10 feet.

WHY IT WORKS: A tamed tree to train
WHERE TO GET IT: thesill.com

44 Pawleys Island Hammock

After Christopher Columbus failed to discover Japan in 1492, this was his consolation prize: the rope hammock, which he brought back from the Bahamas. Devised by islanders as a way to get a good night's sleep while suspended above the peril of snakes and insects, the hammock later joined the British Navy on the high seas. At the end of the eighteenth century, a Southern riverboat captain known as Cap'n Josh tried adding a slat from an oak barrel to each end of the hammock to create a flat bed of woven rope. He preferred this method of sleeping— and so did his neighbors. The hammocks are still woven in Cap'n Josh's hometown of Pawleys Island, South Carolina.

WHY IT WORKS: Structured for extended loafing
WHERE TO GET IT: pawleysislandhammocks.com

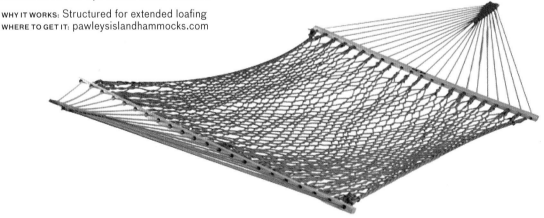

45 Weber Grill

In 1952 George Stephen, a welder (and barbecue aficionado) at the Weber Brothers Metal Works in Chicago, connected the two halves of a metal buoy to create an enclosed and therefore more efficient grill. Little did he know it would soon become an iconic symbol of summertime in America. He poked ventilation holes in the sides and took "George's Barbecue Kettle" on the road to sell to hardware stores across the country. The grills became so popular that George bought the Weber factory.

WHY IT WORKS: The last word in charbroiled taste
WHERE TO GET IT: weber.com

46 Twine Stand

Made in Scotland by Nutscene, this beech twine holder is as indispensable in the potting shed as it is in the kitchen or mudroom. Its heart lies in the thistle shape at the top, which conceals a cutter—no scissors needed. Additionally, the stand allows the ball of Nutscene twine to unravel in an orderly fashion.

WHY IT WORKS: No untangling or looking for scissors
WHERE TO GET IT: ancientindustries.com

47 Baker Creek Herb Seeds

An herb garden is a lovely thing, but like a potager, it is not meant to produce industrial-sized quantities. Yet there are certain flavors we crave daily, including basil, parsley, thyme, and rosemary. For succession planting, sow seeds every four weeks or so—in pots, in garden beds, or, if necessary, in that empty spot beside the kitchen stoop—to ensure a continuous crop. Time-tested varieties are top performers; Baker Creek Heirloom Seed Company sells many seeds dating to the 1800s. Founder Jere Gettle printed his first catalog when he was seventeen, and nearly twenty years later offers more than 1,750 herb, vegetable, and flower seeds.

WHY THEY WORK: Because a meal without fresh herbs isn't a meal
WHERE TO GET THEM: rareseeds.com

48 Mother-in-Law's Tongue Houseplant

We know the air-cleansing benefits of houseplants, trading carbon dioxide for oxygen in closer quarters than their outdoor counterparts. Enter *Sansevieria trifasciata*, which will also absorb formaldehyde (found in bathroom products and tissues) while putting up with life on the floor next to the wastepaper basket. It thrives on shower steam, irregular watering, and any dim lighting you can provide. After all this, mother-in-law's tongue deserves a better common name.

WHY IT WORKS: Nearly indestructible
WHERE TO GET IT: realornamentals.com

49 Succulents

In autumn they buzz with pollinating insects, standing proud as everything collapses around them. And yet they're ignored and forgotten during all the glory months. Succulents have water-retaining glaucous foliage—the pillowy leaves one loves to stroke—which allows them to thrive in drought conditions. Drainage is important, though: too much water and they're dead. Ditto frost: at home in the desert, most succulents need protection in winter, when they are happy to transform into low-maintenance houseplants.

WHY THEY WORK: Best plants to neglect
WHERE TO GET THEM: shopterrain.com

50 Jackson & Perkins Boot Scraper

Discreetly offering itself as a buffer between the muddy outdoors and a well-swept interior, the wrought-iron boot scraper was traditionally made by blacksmiths, its design pleasingly functional. Now that a temptation toward curlicues has infiltrated smiths' designs, it takes some determination to find a scraper that quietly does the job. No installation is required with the Jackson & Perkins model: simply push the sharpened legs straight into the ground.

WHY IT WORKS: All business, no frills
WHERE TO GET IT: jacksonandperkins.com

51 Hunter Gardening Boots

When Lady Diana Spencer was photographed in a pair of Hunter boots after her engagement was announced, it was just the latest in a long history of accolades for the venerable British footwear company (founded by American expat Henry Lee Norris in 1856). Hunter shod British soldiers in the trenches in two world wars, has been awarded a Royal Warrant, and makes a short version of its original buckled Wellington boots that is completely waterproof in the garden—and comes in a range of crayon colors. (Don't think Military Red hasn't tempted us.)

WHY THEY WORK: High-traction grip to stand tall in muck
WHERE TO GET THEM: hunterboots.com

52 Stoneware Jingle Bells

To Tibetan Buddhists, the gentle ringing of a bell is a call to mindfulness. In the garden, Brooklyn-based sculptor Michele Quan's haute hippie jingle bells serve a similar purpose: they "are an homage to the present through sound," she says. Straddling the line between art and ornament, the handmade ceramic pieces look equally happy hanging singly or in clusters, suspended from a tree branch by their heavy hemp cords.

WHY THEY WORK: Call it sculpture or call everyone in to supper
WHERE TO GET THEM: totokaelo.com

53 Recycled Tire Trug

An abandoned car tire from Syria, refashioned into a garden trug, turns out to be as good-looking as it is environmentally friendly. With a hand-stitched and cleated construction and clearly discernible tire tread, the trug projects a handsome sense of style. In addition to being waterproof and impervious to weather, this useful basket for carting plants and compost is equally serviceable for display and storage, indoors or out.

WHY IT WORKS: Upcycled recyclable
WHERE TO GET IT: atelier-home.co.uk

54 Westport Chair

Often referred to as the Adirondack chair (though it answers to the more specific name of Westport), this modernist lounger first appeared in the early twentieth century. Thomas Lee came up with the enforced-loafing design as a response to life in the mountains: the chair's backward tilt and generous armrests challenge any sitter to leap up in a hurry. Various styles that imitate the original all share the same use of wide planks, generally made of wood. This version packs flat.

WHY IT WORKS: Designed for those who make time to slow down
WHERE TO GET IT: jardinique.com (and rhbabyandchild.com, for a child-size version)

55 Roost Hummingbird Feeder

Finally: a clear glass hummingbird feeder that is as captivating to look at as the feathered creatures it attracts. Made of sturdy, laboratory-grade borosilicate glass, each cylindrical feeder has a glass loop from which it can hang from a tree branch (preferably just outside your kitchen window). Headquartered in Sausalito, California (a hotbed of hummingbird activity), designer Roost Home Furnishings took a minimalist approach to creating a simple product that shows off our avian friends to maximum effect. To use the feeder at home, just add sugar water—and enjoy the show.

WHY IT WORKS: Eschews frills and plays up the proper plumage
WHERE TO GET IT: nova68.com

56 Café String Lights

Bistro, patio, terrazzo: whatever you wish to call these outdoor spaces that beckon us on summer nights, the mood is enhanced by the warm light that emanates from overhead. Café string lights are reminiscent of a French fete in summer or nocturnal festivities in winter, and should be used year-round, festooned in the garden or trained like roses around the cottage door. Commercial-grade outdoor lights will last for years.

WHY THEY WORK: Cast a golden glow on summer
WHERE TO GET THEM: napastyle.com

57 Olive Tree Topiary

A lazy person's answer to a topiary shape, potted olive trees give a dramatic effect while remaining loosely "lollipop" in outline, no clipping necessary. Silvery-green leaves reflect the light. Olive fruit is a nonessential bonus. Olives are acclimated to arid conditions and can be neglected within reason (unlike, say, a boxwood topiary).

WHY IT WORKS: A slow grower, happy to be left alone
WHERE TO GET IT: surlatable.com

58 Staghorn Kokedama

Consider this a fusion houseplant, bringing together some of the best aspects of two gardening cultures to create a new kind of plant. Native to rain forests, *Platycerium bifurcatum* (staghorn fern) prefers to grow on trees in filtered sunlight in moist environments, making it the perfect candidate to become a Japanese-style *kokedama*. Wrapped in a moss ball that retains moisture and holds soil in place, a *kokedama* can be suspended from a ceiling or cradled in a saucer. Mist it lightly when you think of it.

WHY IT WORKS: Rain forest meets Japan, and they like each other
WHERE TO GET IT: thesill.com

59 Japanese Hori-Hori

It's you versus weeds, mano a mano. In this battle you need a weapon you can trust. A *hori-hori* (a Japanese farmers' tool named after their word for "dig") has a serrated forged-steel blade to give you the necessary advantage. This is a tool that will cut through roots if it has to. And it has to. With a slight curve to the blade, it also helps you ruthlessly scoop out those roots. Use the knife to divide clumps of strangled perennials, cut blocks of sod, pry weeds from between bricks, or loosen the small but obstructive rocks trying to thwart your plans.

WHY IT WORKS: Never needs sharpening
WHERE TO GET IT: garrettwade.com

60 Casamidy Lantern

Jorge Alameda and Anne-Marie Midi run their furniture design firm, Casamidy, from a home base in San Miguel Allende, Mexico. An American-French husband-and-wife team, they have worked for more than fifteen years with local Mexican artists to create furniture and accessories (with forays into interior design). Their hand-wrought iron lanterns, suitable for both indoor and outdoor use, are offered in a variety of finishes and sizes. The tallest is 36 inches; it has a hand-forged glass door with a little latch you can open to replace candles.

WHY IT WORKS: Simple shapes from south of the border
WHERE TO GET IT: casamidy.com

61 Labour and Wait Leather Work Gloves

There are fiber gloves and rubber gloves, but for durability and comfort, these lined leather gloves can't be beat. They manage perfectly well without high-tech credentials, and considering the soft, high-quality leather used, they are a good value. The fact that they are white may cause amusement in some quarters, but we're not saying they have to stay spotless: dirty white is a badge of honor. The fact is, they are warm in winter and comfortable in summer, not least because of the cotton lining.

WHY THEY WORK: Natural materials for work in natural surroundings
WHERE TO GET THEM: labourandwait.co.uk

62 Mira Copper Trowel

The British company Implementations has a cult following. Biodynamic growers favor its handsome copper-based tools because the metal is electrically conductive and nonmagnetic, and followers believe that using copper tools in the garden helps deter slugs and snails. Visit the company's website to read about the science behind this theory. The Mira trowel is made of bronze (90 percent copper and 10 percent tin), and while it's not as hard as steel, it still lasts at least a generation; Implementations tools come with a twenty-five-year guarantee.

WHY IT WORKS: Shiny superhero in the garden
WHERE TO GET IT: implementations.co.uk

63 Kekkilä Pot Ladder

Install an instant indoor garden. Designers Klaus and Alina Aalto's quest to find new points of view for everyday objects led them to create a foldable, three-tier stepladder to hold plants. Equally at home on a balcony or in the bedroom, the Kekkilä Pot Ladder has a beechwood frame and three removable painted steel shelves that do double duty as drainage trays.

WHY IT WORKS: Small footprint, big impact
WHERE TO GET IT: finnishdesignshop.com

64 Slate Markers

Though the plants in your edible garden will change with the season, the plant markers should endure. Reusable natural slate markers are Prince Charles's choice, both in his private gardens at Highgrove House and at his Highgrove shop (whose profits are donated to a charitable foundation). A set of five locally quarried slate markers comes with an erasable white grease pencil.

WHY THEY WORK: Will weather any weather
WHERE TO GET THEM: highgroveshop.com

65 Davey & Co. Bulkhead Light

Transcending its marine origins, this tough and practical bulkhead light is a combination of die-cast aluminum, prismatic glass, and wire cage—which together give it an extravagantly industrial edge. Hardware and lighting specialist Davey & Co. began furnishing the ships and dockyards of East London in 1885; nowadays the company's focus is domestic lighting, and the components continue to be handmade in England to withstand the worst the sea has to offer. In 2010, Davey was acquired by Original BTC, another byword in the world of quality illumination.

WHY IT WORKS: Classic style, with a midshipman's muscle
WHERE TO GET IT: guideboat.com

66 Kohler Outdoor Shower

It seems fitting that the classic design of this exposed outdoor shower is by Kohler, a Wisconsin-based company with a serious interest in leisure as well as industry. Kohler has had a colorful history, from making torpedo tubes in World War II to contributing parts to the Apollo moon landing. The joy of this design is that it is freestanding, with its solid brass construction open to full view.

WHY IT WORKS: Exposed plumbing with nothing to hide
WHERE TO GET IT: kohler.com

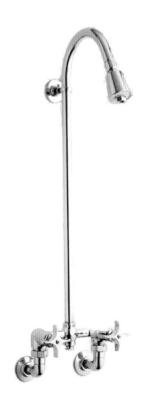

67 Rejuvenation Classic Doorbell

A singsong *ding-dong* is all that's required to accompany a simple round doorbell. It calms the visitor and hints at an ordered life within. An intercom system with camera and buzzer has the opposite effect, and a bell-pull attached to a series of jangling chimes can be just as disconcerting. Accessorize this simple device with a peephole in the door for a visitor preview.

WHY IT WORKS: A moment of sense in the doorbell timeline
WHERE TO GET IT: rejuvenation.com

68 Henry Dean Hurricane Candleholder

Company founder Henri Doyen's first foray into manufacturing involved plastic flowers for funerals, but by 1972 he and his wife, Edith, were exporting glassware from Belgium to lucky neighboring countries. Under the name Henry Dean, the Antwerp-based glassblower has been creating original designs for more than thirty years. Like the rest of the company's offerings, each handmade Tournon Hurricane candleholder begins life as a mixture of sand, soda, and lime. Heated to a glowing red ball of lava at a temperature of 1,500 degrees Celsius, the glass is shaped into a cylinder that gracefully straddles the line between usefulness and beauty. Candlelight is the best cosmetic.

WHY IT WORKS: Light a flame and it's magical
WHERE TO GET IT: marchsf.com

69 Henry Dean Clear Glass Vase

Vases are rarely tall enough, wide enough, or big enough. A jug or pitcher can be a charming alternative—or you can rely on the just-right Belgian-blown Henry Dean Alentejo vase, made of thick glass with no embellishments. The heavy base and wide mouth allow stems to be shown at their best advantage without tipping over.

WHY IT WORKS: Displays cut flowers with no messing about
WHERE TO GET IT: marchsf.com

70 Aigle Garden Clogs

Aigle footwear, instantly recognizable as French because of its great style, was originally made by an American who set up a factory in France. These natural rubber clogs, named after the American eagle, are handmade with a cotton lining and a cork insole. Vulcanization, a technique for curing rubber, is key to their comfort; it was developed by Charles Goodyear, who sold the patent to the founder of Aigle. The two hundred master rubber craftsmen who make each clog and boot the company manufactures are responsible for the perfection of shape and detail.

WHY THEY WORK: Slip-on chic
WHERE TO GET THEM: aigle.com

71 Neutra House Numbers

Neutraface has all the sleek and elegant qualities of a font designed in the 1930s. It practically shouts California: Hollywood, modernism, and glass houses. Richard Neutra, designer of many glass houses, is the inspiration for Neutraface. Designer Christian Schwartz, who worked with Neutra's son to design a font that encapsulated the principles of the man, created this one in 2002. House Industries released Neutraface to instant acclaim and, with Heath Ceramics, decided to apply the architecture-inspired font to architecture.

WHY THEY WORK: California modernism distilled in a number
WHERE TO GET THEM: heathceramics.com

72 Feuerhand Hurricane Lantern

After being put to good use on long summer nights, a kerosene lamp will segue nicely into hurricane season. Made in Germany by Feuerhand since 1902, the hurricane lantern is safely sealed against spillage, and has thermal glass to balance the heat it emits against rain or even snow outside. It emits an ambient glow associated with an earlier era (sans soot).

WHY IT WORKS: Takes the fear out of storms
WHERE TO GET IT: lanternnet.com

73 Pointer Waist Apron

L. C. King was a manufacturer and hunter who named a clothing line after his favorite dog breed. Since 1913, Pointer Brand has produced American workwear of the denim, hickory-striped, and brown duck cotton varieties in its family-owned factory in Bristol, Tennessee. The waist aprons are particularly genius as they are the right length for gardening; apron pockets keep tools handy without getting in the way when you kneel.

WHY IT WORKS: Keeps the essentials in arm's reach
WHERE TO GET IT: pointerbrand.com

74 French Enamel House Numbers

Around the time that Baron Haussmann was reorganizing Paris, street signs and house numbers got reconsidered as well. With a resilient surface of ground glass, the porcelain enamel sign could withstand the various weather conditions of this northern city, as well as the vigor of city life. Enamel signs were until then made only in black and white. We don't know who decided to add chromium dioxide as a color pigment, but the result was a shade of ultramarine easily spotted across a wide boulevard. The blue *vêtements de travail*, or French work uniforms, followed suit, and blue became the color of efficiency in France.

WHY THEY WORK: Functional French at its best
WHERE TO GET THEM: ramsign.com

75 Woven Rattan Backpack

Though it may have started in life as a market and fruit-picking pack, we see so much more potential when we gaze at this hard-sided carryall. We see summer in its entirety: Picnic basket. Beach bag. Market tote. The possibilities are glorious. Made of woven Malaysian rattan (sustainably harvested) with a cotton handle and adjustable leather shoulder straps, the backpack has a reinforced wooden base made of ash. No sandwich will get smashed on its watch.

WHY IT WORKS: Natural fibers, no end to its usefulness
WHERE TO GET IT: kaufmann-mercantile.com

76 U.S. Mailbox

Back when the fire and police departments were rival factions, the U.S. Mail was in similar disarray. Rural routes were dotted with handmade mailboxes that did not necessarily fare well in snow, rain, or sleet. In 1915, postal engineer Roy Joroleman designed a standard mailbox: essentially an oversize tin can with a latched door and a flat base for a post. Beyond the addition of the jaunty red flag, the classic mailbox has barely changed over the years. It remains a symbol of domestic American life in all terrains and climates.

WHY IT WORKS: An American icon still made in America
WHERE TO GET IT: gibraltarmailboxes.com

77 Garrett Wade Sharpest Shovel

To love tools is a kind of religion. Feel it when your palm touches the cool, confident handle of this sharp-bladed, all-steel shovel. New York–based tool seller Garrett Wade, whose company founder insists that every item for sale be as useful as the well-made woodworking tools he loved as a boy, offers a range of 1,700; to get on that list, the Super Penetration Shovel proved its worth with a tapered, pointed blade and sharpened sides. It can break up clay and heavily compacted soil, and comes with a detachable rubber footrest to give a gardener even greater leverage.

WHY IT WORKS: Gives you the advantage on tricky terrain
WHERE TO GET IT: garrettwade.com

78 Eena Garden Tote

It's not surprising that Pacific Northwest camping specialist Beckel Canvas (the same company that has been making high-quality canvas tents and lean-tos for fifty years) came up with the ideal garden tool bag. In collaboration with their Portland, Oregon, neighbors at Canoe, Beckel's designers have created a heavy canvas bucket with a water-repellent vinyl base and capacious interior. Named the Eena Garden Tote in reference to the Chinook *eena* ("the beaver who builds the best house"), the bag makes a stout home for tools.

WHY IT WORKS: Sturdy marries style in the garden
WHERE TO GET IT: canoeonline.net

79 Marine Light

In wind and rain, this atmospheric light hints at distant shipwrecks. Variously known as a harbor sconce, wharf sconce, or ship's well glass light, a marine lamp has a steadfast beam that should prove to be "squall-proof, embracing bad weather with gusto." The bronze fixture has a seeded glass dome, as if it needed any more romance.

WHY IT WORKS: Protected illumination for a porch, veranda, or foggy sea
WHERE TO GET IT: circalighting.com

80 Niwaki Ladder

It may be hard to imagine having a close relationship with a climbing aid, but the Japanese tripod ladder is very lovable. It's light, yet large and stable. Made from extruded aluminum, it has a telescopic leg that can be adjusted for sloping ground. Or you can forget the tripod and lean the whole thing against a wall. The base is wide enough for even the most trepidatious pruner to ascend without fear, because a climber's weight pushes it downward and outward.

WHY IT WORKS: There is joy both in using and carrying it
WHERE TO GET IT: niwaki.com

81 Galvanized Funnel

Many of us improvise for years, when a small but vital purchase—a funnel—could simplify countless tasks. Suddenly, all is flowing. Liquid plant feed—whether it's homemade comfrey tea, the by-product of a wormery, or something store-bought—is better poured through a galvanized funnel. Filling many bird feeders is almost impossible without a funnel, and yet most of us do it, spilling a feast for the ground-bound creatures.

WHY IT WORKS: Survivor from ancient times simplifies modern chores
WHERE TO GET IT: plews-edelmann.com

82 Folding Deck Chair

The low-slung teak deck chair has its origins in sea travel, but the English also associate it with park seating, paid for by the hour. In the UK, one's local council dictated the livery of its deck chairs, in suitably dour colors for the austerity years. With brighter fabric colors reminiscent of Provençal sunshine, the alter ego of this foldaway chair comes to the fore. We see why the 150-year-old French company Les Toiles du Soleil only does bright and bold.

WHY IT WORKS: More than temporary seating
WHERE TO GET IT: lestoilesdusoleilnyc.com

83 Felco Pruners

Unsurprisingly, the most efficient and mechanically inspired pruning shears in the world are Swiss. Red-handled and brilliantly designed, Felco pruners are as distinctive as the Swiss Army knife, having been developed with global ambitions since the 1940s. Rotating handles were introduced early, decades before RSI (repetitive stress injury) became a watchword. In addition to practical durability, Felco embraces the idea of service, citing "respect" and "humility" among its core values. It is a rare garden professional who does not carry a pair at all times.

WHY THEY WORK: Ergonomic design and a quality cut
WHERE TO GET THEM: felcousa.com

84 Alabax Light

Pass & Seymour's American Alabax dominated domestic lighting in the first half of the twentieth century. The ageless combination of exposed bulbs and simple porcelain shapes is still appealing, not least on the porch—which is why Schoolhouse Electric has named its own timeless shapes in honor of the American classics, with porcelain parts made in Portland, Oregon.

WHY IT WORKS: Makes twentieth-century American style seem timeless
WHERE TO GET IT: schoolhouseelectric.com

85 Pendleton Roll-Up Picnic Blanket

The mere name of this family-owned American mill evokes images of autumn plaid. Virgin wool blankets have been made for more than a hundred years in the town of Pendleton, Oregon, woven in traditional Scottish tartans or American plaids. This picnic blanket measures a generous 60 by 70 inches and has a convenient handle for carrying. Kept in the car trunk, it's a call to spontaneous fun.

WHY IT WORKS: Sensible waterproof backing for year-round use
WHERE TO GET IT: pendleton-usa.com

86 Striptable

At the heart of Dutch designer Piet Hein Eek's enormous, light-filled studio in Eindhoven, Netherlands, is the factory where he oversees every step of the process of creating his beautifully imagined collection of furniture and lighting. There is drama and weight to his teak Striptable, a piece of furniture that honors the communal act of dining with friends. With perfect proportions and a heavy galvanized steel base, this is a table that reminds you a meal is more than a menu; it's the ritual that ties us together.

WHY IT WORKS: Museum worthy, but more concerned about your comfort
WHERE TO GET IT: thefutureperfect.com, pietheineek.nl/en

87 Best Made Axe

With twenty-eight styles on its books (at last count), New York City's Best Made Company would appear to have something of an axe fetish. Each Hudson Bay axe comes with a bridle-leather blade guard and embroidered badge, all nestled in a handmade wooden box—appealing to collectors as well as to those who simply want to chop wood or clear brush. Not really complete without a duck canvas axe case.

WHY IT WORKS: Fast track to the frontier
WHERE TO GET IT: bestmadeco.com

88 Great Dixter Trowel

The Dutch take gardening aids very seriously, and none more so than Jaap Sneeboer and Wilma Peleen, purveyors of indispensable garden tools of sharpened steel. A desire for modern-day efficiency mixed with a curiosity about traditional tools has given Sneeboer a unique aesthetic. The Great Dixter trowel is an excellent example: designed to the exacting specifications of the estate's owner, Christopher Lloyd, it became one of the renowned twentieth-century English gardener's best-loved hand tools. Indispensable both for putting plants into and coaxing them out of the soil, the trowel's narrow blade fits into the tightest cracks to pull out weeds. Its length achieves admirable depth when it's time to plant seedlings.

WHY IT WORKS: A sharp, hand-forged tool that makes stainless steel seem very dull
WHERE TO GET IT: sneeboer.com

89 Filson Log Carrier

"Might as well have the best" is the Filson motto, and who are we to disagree? Responding to the Great Klondike Gold Rush of 1897, C. C. Filson used his experience of outfitting loggers in Seattle to accommodate the ill-equipped prospectors stampeding north. The company continues to produce quality American clothing for outdoor activities, specializing in oiled canvas. This material is also used for the log carrier, which is strengthened with sewn and riveted handles made of bridle leather.

WHY IT WORKS: Handsome and rugged
WHERE TO GET IT: filson.com

90 Coir Bootscraper Doormat

Coir, a hardy fiber made from coconut husk, is used for ropes, brushes, and floor matting. Combined with steel wire, it produces a stiff surface that effectively scrapes off mud and resists moisture. Handmade in India, this durable doormat has an underside of recycled rubber and blends unobtrusively with its surroundings.

WHY IT WORKS: Natural and long-lasting
WHERE TO GET IT: wayfair.com

91 Model A Tolix Chair

French sheet-metal manufacturer Xavier Pauchard (the son and grandson of zinc roofers) had a breakthrough when he discovered that dipping metal in zinc created a weatherproof galvanized finish. He began selling his galvanized metal chair (and gave the design his trademarked Tolix name) in 1934. The stackable Tolix chair has in the ensuing decades sailed across the sea on the decks of the S.S. *Normandie*, become the world's most iconic café-style chair, and joined MoMA's permanent collection of twentieth-century design. To this day, the chair is manufactured of sheet metal in the Burgundy factory town of Autun.

WHY IT WORKS: Oft-copied, never improved upon
WHERE TO GET IT: dwr.com

92 Campo de' Fiori Aged Victorian Planter

Classic terra-cotta has long been a mainstay of the respectably well-dressed garden, and planters from Campo de' Fiori, based in the Berkshires of Massachusetts, have a mossy patina so convincing it might have been acquired in your great-grandmother's garden. Or Queen Victoria's. The design, with a drainage hole on the side, originated at her holiday estate, Balmoral Castle, where Campo de' Fiori owners Robin Norris and Barbara Brockbader won the right to reproduce it "after a poker game."

WHY IT WORKS: The little black dress of the garden, terra-cotta goes with everything
WHERE TO GET IT: grdnbklyn.com, campodefiori.com

93 Lead-Free Garden Hose

Now that skipping through a sprinkler comes with a health warning (as the material of most garden hoses contains lead, PBA, and phthalates), we need to find ways to preserve simple pleasures. It's safe to drink out of the hose if it comes from American manufacturers Water Right; the company specializes in polyurethane hoses free of toxins. In addition, the hoses are lightweight and easy to maneuver. Happily, they also come in nontraditional colors, including gunmetal and eggplant.

WHY IT WORKS: American summers restored
WHERE TO GET IT: waterrightinc.com

94 Barn Light Electric Warehouse Light

Barn light, church light, store light: the familiar gooseneck shape from Barn Light Electric gives any building a glowing sense of twentieth-century Americana. With a graceful arc of an arm, it beckons you home at nightfall. Galvanized is the traditional finish, though choices from blush pink to emerald green are also available—all American-made.

WHY IT WORKS: Gives pools of Edward Hopper–quality light
WHERE TO GET IT: barnlightelectric.com

95 Go Porch Swing

A wide porch with a wooden swing is a wonderful combination, though neither "wide" nor "wooden" is really essential. The Go porch swing, a modern version by Loll Designs, is made in the United States from recycled milk jugs. At 52 inches wide, it can hang in a smaller porch while offering the same joys of swinging, talking, and sipping. It comes in a range of desirable shiny colors, and requires no special maintenance to remain outdoors.

WHY IT WORKS: Friendly (toward people and the earth)
WHERE TO GET IT: dwr.com

96 Burgon & Ball Herb Shears

Made in Sheffield, the home of English steel manufacture, the blades on these cutters are a smaller version of the renowned sheep shears. A handier pair of snips for shearing the tops off herbs, or going in for specific cuts, they are made from bespoke high-carbon British steel, their blades hot-forged and heat-treated. Keep them by the back door but well out of weather's way.

WHY THEY WORK: Cutting power for your pocket
WHERE TO GET THEM: shovelandhoe.com

97 Clay Window Box

The manufacture of terra-cotta has been associated with the region around Florence for thousands of years. Wood-fired kilns similar to those used in Roman times are still put to use in many Italian potteries. In the mid-1990s, Seibert & Rice opened lines of trade with Impruneta, the sine qua non of terra-cotta production in Tuscany, to create a classically shaped terra-cotta window box that is remarkably frost-resistant.

WHY IT WORKS: Rosy-hued, hardy, and beautiful in old age
WHERE TO GET IT: seibert-rice.com

98 Wood-Handled Dustpan

A tidy hardscape is the unglamorous secret of a successful garden. For all the complex planting and thorough weeding, a neat edge and a well-swept path will always count for more. To do the job, arm yourself with equipment that is not itself banal: the wooden handle, little leather loop, and sensible rubber lip will all improve the experience.

WHY IT WORKS: German enthusiasm for tidiness
WHERE TO GET IT: brookfarmgeneralstore.com

99 Ron Rezek Ceiling Fan

Before the invention of a water-based air-conditioning system in mid-nineteenth-century North America, those who could afford it made do in summer with servant-operated punkahs, or slowly flapping fabric fans. In the 1880s, Philip Diehl invented the ceiling fan. He employed a sewing machine motor and soon attached a light fixture as well. Since the 1920s the fortunes of the ceiling fan have fluctuated, as the allure of air-conditioning sidelined it temporarily. These days, its energy-saving qualities contribute to an ever-growing appeal. Ron Rezek's design is in sync with its industrial roots and creates a cooling breeze on a sticky day.

WHY IT WORKS: Screened porch must-have
WHERE TO GET IT: ylighting.com

100 Great States Push Mower

An earth-friendly push mower, requiring no gas, makes a finer cut than a power mower. It also makes you more popular if you live next door to someone who doesn't love the sound of a roaring engine wafting over the hedges. Keep the blades sharpened and keep the peace in the neighborhood.

WHY IT WORKS: Quiet, nonpolluting, and easily stored
WHERE TO GET IT: americanlawnmower.com

Expert Advice

LANDSCAPE AND GARDEN DESIGN

If you're anything like us, garden work is always more balm than toil. But when it comes to overhauling an outdoor space, calling in a pro is sometimes well advised. In this chapter we've culled wisdom from landscape professionals and from our own experiences (several of us at Gardenista have lived through the muddy trenches to tell about it). We'll help guide you from beginning to end, punch list included.

By Jean Victor

01

Before You Dig In

This is the time to dream big—you can rein in your wildest ideas later, if need be. Start by making a list of everything you want in your outdoor space, even if the list is a mile long. Then use the following key considerations to separate the musts from the maybes.

WISH LIST

How do you want to live in your outdoor space? What kinds of activities would you like to indulge in? Do you want an outdoor dining room with seating for eight? A fire pit to extend fall evenings beyond dusk? Write it all down. Then prioritize the list.

STYLE AND AESTHETIC

How do you want your landscape to look and how do you want to feel in it? Gather images of garden spaces you love, with an eye to style, colors, materials, plants, and furniture. Websites are an ideal place to start. Gardenista.com is full of inspiration, and it's all organized by category, from urban gardens to outdoor furniture.

Take note—or better yet, photos—of gardens you admire in your neighborhood or on your travels. Leaf through design magazines and books. Put together a physical binder of images as well as an online file on Pinterest. As you do so, you're bound to see certain styles or themes emerge.

Perhaps you're drawn to English country gardens drenched in green, or modern landscapes with simple lines. Is there a lot of stonework in the gardens you like, or particular color schemes or types of plants? After you have a clear direction, take stock of the images and delete any that don't fit.

BUDGET

Decide on a "not to exceed" dollar amount. If you're working with a landscape architect or designer, give him or her a clear idea of your budget at the start, so the project can be designed within your parameters. See how much of your wish list can be included in the master plan; you can always scale back. Or use the master plan as a goal to work toward in phases.

Budgets matter on more than one level. You want to be realistic about how much you can spend, and you also want to get the best value for your money in terms of cost and quality. According to the Association of Professional Landscape Designers, spending 5 to 10 percent of your home's value on a basic, well-designed landscape can reap as much as 200 percent in return. If your house is worth $500,000, for example, this translates into spending $25,000 to $50,000 to see its value increase an average of $50,000 to $100,000. *Basic* and *well designed* are the key words here; the numbers vary widely depending on the scale and scope of your project. Splurge-worthy items such as mature trees, stonework, or an outdoor kitchen will increase the cost but could add even more to the property value in the end.

SUSTAINABILITY

If an environmentally friendly landscape is a priority (as it should be), put that at the top of your wish list. It will influence everything from building materials and plant selection to irrigation and maintenance.

MAINTENANCE LEVEL

Keeping a garden in good shape requires time and money. Be realistic about how much of both you're willing to spend. Are you an avid gardener or do you prefer to just mow and occasionally weed? Are you planning to hire a gardener for seasonal planting and pruning, or do you want a team to come by every week? If low maintenance is a must, lean toward an easygoing landscape that requires minimal care. Your design team can let you know up front if the items on your list are in line with the maintenance level you want.

SITING AND ARCHITECTURE

Take cues from the siting and architectural style of your house. First, consider the physical characteristics of your site. Is it flat or sloped? Which areas get sun and which are shady? These considerations affect the design and the cost. Tip: Working with the natural lay of the land almost always has a lower price tag.

If your home's style is traditional, try complementing it with clean, modern garden lines. If the house is contemporary, soften it with curving beds and pathways. Look at the axis from your front or back door or a favorite window and see where your eye falls. Load that point with something special—an amazing tree or garden ornament. Pick up on the house's exterior materials, such as stone or brick, and repeat them somewhere in the landscape.

CLIMATE AND SEASONALITY

Obviously, the climate where you live will determine which plants you can grow. Check the USDA Plant Hardiness Zone map online to find out your climate zone. The map is based on the average annual extreme minimum temperature, and it will give you an idea of which plants can thrive in your area. Jasmine and citrus trees won't survive freezing winters, for example, while tulips struggle to make a yearly comeback in temperate climates. If you

have four seasons, design for year-round interest—spring and summer blooms, fall color, winter silhouettes. If you live in the desert, consider well-placed containers that can take up the slack when plants go dormant.

SOIL

Find out the type of soil native to where you live and determine its condition in different parts of your garden. (Landscape architects and designers usually include soil testing in the scope of their work.) Soil conditions will influence plant selection and tell you how much drainage work needs to be done.

ZONING AND PERMITS

Depending on the scope of your project, you may need to apply for building approval or permits. A new deck or arbor, a retaining wall over a certain height, and grading that affects drainage patterns are just a few of the items that can require approvals or permits. Estimate the time it will take to get them and add that to your schedule. (Unless you're going it alone, your design team or contractor will likely obtain these for you.)

02

Where to Splurge, Where to Save

Many of the elements used to create an outdoor space can feel costly up front but will save you money in the long run. Installing a superefficient irrigation system, for example, is pricey but pays off in reduced water bills. Quality materials and craftsmanship withstand the elements longer. Thorough soil preparation saves you from having to replace plants that don't thrive. That said, here's our take on the best ways to mix up big gestures with more affordable options.

TEN THINGS WORTH SPENDING ON

❶ A master plan.
Don't go at a landscape project piecemeal or without a clear direction. Spend the money up front to have a landscape architect or designer create a master plan of where you want your garden to be in five or ten years, then use that as a road map to work toward in phases, as your budget allows.

❷ Masonry.
Stone and brickwork are big-ticket items, but masonry retaining walls, terraces, steps, and paths add timeless beauty to a landscape. They also give your garden good bones throughout the seasons: in a cold climate, when the garden takes a winter rest, the underlying structure of stone provides continuing visual interest amid a color palette of browns and grays.

❸ A great view.
If something interferes with a beautiful view in your outdoor space, pay to have that something removed. Transplant a tree to another location, for example, or bury power lines.

❹ Quality materials that withstand the elements.
Natural stone, wrought iron, steel, copper, teak, redwood, cedar, ipe: quality materials such as these not only last longer but are also enhanced by the elements. Some woods (teak, redwood, cedar) mellow to a silvery gray over time, metals acquire a patina, and stone takes on a veil of moss. Pressure-treated lumber may be less expensive, but it tends to warp.

❺ Craftsmanship.
Building anything well requires careful attention to detail, whether it's laying flagstone on a patio, forming concrete for a retaining wall, or sinking fence posts. You'll quickly notice the difference between high-quality and so-so workmanship.

❻ Soil preparation.
Good soil is the basis of a healthy garden. Have it tested early on so you know your soil type—sandy, loamy, clay. Spend the money to address any deficiencies by adding soil amendments or even replacing bad or toxic soil.

❼ A one-of-a-kind specimen tree.
Even if you've decided to save money by purchasing smaller plants for most of the garden, splurge on a special tree in a larger container, such as a 36-inch box.

❽ Fencing or green walls for privacy.
If privacy is a priority, invest in a well-designed wooden fence. Or build a screen by planting a high hedge.

❾ A gorgeous piece of outdoor furniture.
A great teak or stone table instantly extends the square footage of a house beyond the threshold and all but invites a weekend brunch or dinner party. If you entertain frequently, choose the most generously sized table your space allows. Also worth the splurge: an outdoor sofa as comfy as the one indoors.

❿ Fire and heat.
Install an exterior heat source to keep your patio or deck comfy when cool temperatures try to chase you inside. The glow of a flame, whether wood- or gas-induced, also adds to the ambience. Or keep the space toasty by tucking radiant heaters in a trellis overhead.

TEN WAYS TO SAVE

❶ Don't toss; transform.
Avoid the temptation to rip out and discard everything in your existing landscape. Take an inventory of existing features and reuse as many of them as you can. Repurpose bricks from a planter for a new pathway; use old fence pickets to make a gate; dig up hardy perennials and move them to a new bed.

❷ Minimize intervention.
Unless you have to change the grade for drainage or some other reason, work with the natural lay of the land and accentuate its positives. It's pricey to build a raised dining terrace where one doesn't exist, for example, or to haul out soil to level an area for a lawn.

❸ Make clever compromises.
Ongoing maintenance costs should be a line item in every budget. If you live in a dry climate but want the English garden look, you'll continually pay for it in high water and upkeep bills. But you don't necessarily have to do either/or. Go ahead and plant roses, for instance, but cut down on the maintenance requirements by planting them in front of an evergreen hedge.

❹ Buy smaller plants.
Patience pays off. Larger plants reap instant gratification, but in a few years those one-gallon containers of pittosporum you bought by the dozen for a hedge will have caught up to their more costly five- or ten-gallon cousins—and likely be healthier to boot. Don't confine yourself to brick-and-mortar plant stores; peruse nursery catalogs online for perennials. The plants will arrive tiny, but they'll soon establish themselves.

❺ Go on a treasure hunt.
Scavenge architectural salvage yards, antiques stores, and junk shops for vintage iron gates, weathered bricks, rustic fence boards, stone troughs, café chairs, column fragments, sculptures, and watering cans. Found items not only save you money but also add a one-of-a-kind touch.

❻ Mix and match furniture.
The cost of outdoor furniture can be overwhelming—but you don't have to buy a matching set. Mix it up by pairing that gorgeous teak table you splurged on with bistro chairs from IKEA.

❼ Take advantage of end-of-season bargains.
Most nurseries have big plant sales in the fall, with markdowns of 50 percent or more. This is also one of the best times of year to plant perennials, trees, shrubs, grasses, bulbs, and even some seeds. The soil is still warm enough to allow root systems to get established, while the cooler temperatures and rain reduce the need to water.

❽ Swap with neighbors.
Fall is the season to divide many perennials and grasses. Ask your neighbors for a clump of the asters or black-eyed Susans you've been admiring in their garden, and in return give them some of your bearded iris (or a basket of apples from your tree).

❾ Make a temporary path.
If a stone path is on your wish list but out of your current budget, don't despair. Simply design for it and then lay down pea gravel, or straw for a more relaxed look, until you're ready to pave. Who knows, you might like the look so much that it becomes permanent.

❿ Leave space for future ornaments.
You don't have to nix that expensive cast-stone sculpture you have your eye on. Just build a placeholder until you can afford it—perhaps an artfully balanced pile of rocks (à la Andy Goldsworthy) or a well-shaped piece of driftwood.

PRO TIP

The Perfect Tree

"If you can afford only a single mature specimen tree, make it one that works for the garden in every season. For example, a dove tree, crabapple, cherry, fringe, or magnolia brings blossoms in the spring, shade in the summer, color in the fall, and a striking silhouette come winter."

—JANELL DENLER HOBART, landscape architect,
Denler Hobart Gardens

03

Small Details, Big Impact

Even the smallest touches can work instant magic on an outdoor space. One carefully considered move and presto, that slightly shabby back fence you're not ready to replace all but disappears. Here are some micro-moves that can make a big difference.

A Cultivated Pot

Even when your garden needs taming, one well-tended pot can make everything else look deliberate. Fill a container with annuals or an evergreen shrub such as boxwood or inkberry and position it near the front porch, say, or on the back patio.

A Restrained Plant Palette

A kaleidoscope of plant colors dizzies the eye instead of calming it. Let the landscape be primarily green and use color as an accent.

Scale and Proportion

It might seem counterintuitive, but when you size your dining and seating areas generously, you make a small outdoor space appear bigger. A classic rule of thumb is to allow a minimum distance from the edge of the table to the nearest obstruction (say, a wall) of 36 inches.

A Good Pruning

Like a great haircut, a good pruning can dramatically change an outdoor space. Do it yourself if you're plant-savvy, or hire a skilled gardener or arborist.

Moving Water

It's easier than you'd think to get the soothing sound of a fountain. You need a simple watertight vessel (say, a terra-cotta pot, a galvanized washtub, or an urn from the salvage yard), a recirculating pump, and an electrical outlet to plug it into.

Basic Black

If you're installing wooden deer fencing, trellises for roses, or stakes for plants, paint those elements black. Black disappears into the garden; that "landscape green" color looks anything but natural.

Complementary Hardscape Materials

Less is more. Make sure your hardscape materials—stone, pavers, gravel, concrete, wood, paint—all work together, and also complement your house's architectural materials.

An Eye to the Edges

Any place where two materials meet is a loaded situation. Pay extra attention to detail and craftsmanship wherever paving meets gravel or a retaining wall, at the corners of raised planting beds, or along the line between lawn and flower bed. Make those junctures as clean as possible—without, need we say, the use of cheap plastic edging.

Fragrance

Citrus trees, jasmine, lilies, roses, lilacs, lemon verbena, mock orange, flowering tobacco, daffodils, honeysuckle, linden trees: the list of fragrant plants is endless, and so is the simple pleasure of a sweet scent on a warm breeze.

A Classic Mailbox

So everyday that it's easy to overlook design-wise, a handsome mailbox adds curb appeal. Replace your dinged or dumpy box with one in a material and style that works with your architecture.

A Well-Swept Path

A good sweeping makes everything look ordered, even if the rest of the garden is leaning toward wild.

04

Getting
(Environmentally)
Friendly

What is a "sustainable garden design"? An eco-friendly garden is one that's friendly to birds, wildlife, and insects as well as to humans. Use water wisely, while remembering that the sound of a recirculating fountain and the perfume of properly irrigated flowers are signs of a local eco-system that is contributing to the well-being of everyone who lives in the garden.

Shrink or Rethink the Lawn
According to the National Wildlife Federation, up to 70 percent of residential water is used in landscaping, and most of it to water lawns. Consider shrinking the lawn or replacing it entirely with mowable native grasses, a permeable surface such as decomposed granite or gravel, or artificial turf—the newest products are much more natural in look and feel.

Limit Intervention
Keep as much of the existing vegetation as possible. The less you disturb the landscape, the more intact the existing ecosystem will remain. If your project includes new house construction, put the building as close to the old location as possible to minimize site work.

Make Sensible Plant Selections
Choose native, drought-tolerant plants, or plants suited to your climate and the conditions in your garden—particularly sun, shade, and soil type. The goal is to help plants establish themselves and reach the point where they need very little supplemental water.

Drain Responsibly
Proper drainage limits the amount of wastewater that disappears into the black hole of storm drains, overloading sewer systems and creeks and streams. To make surfaces permeable wherever possible, avoid large slabs of concrete or paved areas with mortar joints.

Install a Superefficient Irrigation System
Unless your irrigation system is state-of-the-art, running it on autopilot can use as much as 50 percent more water than necessary. Look for a system with the newest "smart" technology (multiple start times, a weather station, evapotranspiration controls, soil sensors) that takes into account the length of the day, temperature, humidity, and rainfall. Or hire an irrigation specialist to audit and repair your existing system.

Welcome Wildlife
Contribute to the health of your garden and the surrounding ecosystem by choosing plants that attract butterflies, bees, and hummingbirds. Replenish the birdbath when it goes dry; hang bird feeders from trellises and trees. If you grow herbs, let some of them flower (basil and thyme, for example) to sweeten the pot for winged visitors.

Add a Working Garden Element

A kitchen garden, potted herbs, fruit trees, beehives, and chicken coops all help you sustain a healthier, more intimate relationship with your garden. Plant a traditional potager—a kitchen garden that combines vegetables and herbs with a cutting garden, thus providing edibles as well as fresh-cut flowers for vases indoors. The vegetables you harvest will save you a few car trips to the market, and the flowers will need to travel only a few feet, rather than the hundreds or thousands of miles cut flowers often do. Use efficient irrigation to balance the extra water needs of edibles.

Go to Seed

Balance a higher water-use area in your garden by taking another area off the irrigation system. Seed it in the fall with a meadow mix suited to your climate, and then let Mother Nature go to work. Winter rains will bring spring and summer flowers, which will go to seed again come fall, starting the cycle all over again.

Source Local Stone

Buy from nearby stone yards for walls, paths, and other masonry work, or find stone that requires the shortest shipping distance.

Use Only Sustainably Harvested or Reclaimed Wood

If you're building a deck or fence from redwood, cedar, or ipe, or buying outdoor teak furniture, look for wood certified as sustainably harvested by the Forest Stewardship Council (FSC). Or source reclaimed wood, which already wears the patina of time.

Plant a Green Roof

If your project includes new building (a garden shed or pool house, for example), consider turning a flat roof green. Consult an engineer; if your roof can support the weight of soil and plants, the benefits are many: more green space for capturing air pollutants, a habitat for birds and bees, reduced runoff, and a great view from an upstairs window. To keep it simple, seed your roof with a native meadow mix and let the rainy season do the rest.

Recapture Garden Water

Every drop counts, even the small amount captured in a rain barrel and used to water container plants. A more effective option, though not for the faint of budget, is a complete system for capturing, filtering, and reusing garden water. Consult a landscape professional with experience in sustainable irrigation to see if this option is worth it on your site.

Go Organic

For the health of all garden residents, stick to organic soil amendments and compost. If you find you can keep a plant healthy only by using a chemical fertilizer or pesticide, it's probably not the right plant for your landscape.

Micromanage the Lawn

Mow grass to a height of 2½ to 3 inches to decrease water demands. Aerate the lawn before and after summer to improve drainage and runoff and allow more water to reach the roots. And water during the cool part of the day (from 3 a.m. to 8 a.m.) and when the air is still to reduce evaporation.

Mulch

A 2-inch layer of mulch can cut down on water evaporation by as much as 75 percent—and also keep weeds to a minimum. Arbor mulch is one good option; it's made from recycled trees and looks natural.

Set Up a Compost Bin

Or, if you're short on space, a compost tumbler. Throw in kitchen scraps and yard waste, sprinkle it liberally with water, and use it as a soil amendment after it's well seasoned.

Ditch the Gas Lawn Mower

According to the EPA, an hour of gas mower use emits as much air pollution as driving a car two hundred miles. Push mowers are great for small lawns; just don't let the grass get too high between cuttings. For larger lawns, cordless electric, solar, and robotic models are other options. Check the EPA website for air or water agencies in your state that have gas lawn mower exchange programs. They often offer new electric models at a reduced price.

Sweep Rather Than Hose

Use a broom and a little muscle rather than a hose and water to clean off driveways, paths, decks, and patios.

Group Plants by Water Needs

Grouping plants with similar water requirements makes it easier to set up zones in your irrigation system.

The New Green

"Brown used to be a more acceptable garden color before irrigation became so popular. Now everyone expects a green lawn. But native grasses are a great option. You just put down native grass seed or plugs, water it to get it going the first year, and let it adapt to the environment. I mow paths through it like a meadow. It's never going to look like Kentucky bluegrass, but it can be really beautiful."

—TIM CALLIS, landscape designer,
DBA Flower Power

05

The Process

If you know your plants and have a strong back, you can easily prep new beds, build a fence, or even install simple drip irrigation. But if your plan involves paving a patio or building a deck, you may want to call in a landscape contractor; and if it enters more complex territory that requires drainage, grading, lighting, or masonry, the services of a design professional are invaluable. Here is some basic advice on choosing a team and what you can expect in the process of making your ideas a reality.

THE TEAM: LANDSCAPE DESIGN PROFESSIONALS

The skills of landscape architects and landscape designers overlap in many areas. The main differences between the two are professional training and an emphasis on hardscape design versus horticulture, though this can vary widely.

If you opt for full service, both landscape architects and landscape designers will work with you from concept through installation. They will also help with the important task of finding the most suitable landscape contractor to implement their designs. Many also offer services after the project is completed, if you need advice or help with ongoing maintenance. If your project involves new house construction or a remodel with exterior components (such as a new deck or terrace, an outdoor kitchen, or a swimming pool), your architect will likely include these hardscape elements in the scope of the work, and will consult with the landscape team to create a seamless vision for the house and garden.

Here's a rundown of what the different pros do.

Landscape architects are highly trained professionals who usually hold either undergraduate or advanced degrees in landscape architecture and have passed a rigorous state licensing exam. They can provide you with a master plan and all necessary construction drawings for a project, including the plans needed to obtain building approvals and permits when necessary.

Landscape designers often hold degrees in design or plant-related areas such as horticulture or botany. They focus on garden design and plant selection. Like landscape architects, they can provide you with a master plan, but if technical drawings are required, they typically work in association with the project's landscape contractor, architect, or civil or structural engineer to provide them.

Landscape contractors oversee the construction and installation process and usually bring in subcontractors—such as structural engineers, electricians, masons, concrete contractors, irrigation specialists, and painters—to implement the more specialized components of the project. If you're thinking about going this design/build route, make sure you check their references carefully and visit a few of their finished projects. Check the contractors' license board in your state to confirm that the landscape contractor is licensed and insured.

WHAT THEY CHARGE

Design fees vary widely, but landscape architects and designers typically charge in one of two ways: hourly, with an estimated total fee based on a percentage of the completed project cost; or by a flat fee for the design phase and hourly after the drawings are completed. Hourly fees during the construction and installation phase typically include such ongoing services as overseeing the contractor to make sure the project is being built to the specifications, managing any issues that might arise, doing soil tests, and sourcing and selecting the plants. For full-service design help, the total fees might run roughly from 10 to 15 percent of the completed project cost. Landscape contractors also usually charge a percentage of the construction costs, again in the 10 to 15 percent range.

THE HIRING PROCESS

As with any professional doing work for you, landscape architects and designers need to be properly vetted. Here's how to find the perfect match.

Start with Referrals

Gather names from friends or acquaintances with landscaping projects you admire. Get recommendations from an architect or a contractor. Find projects on the web or in magazines you like and consult the companies' websites to get an idea of their overall aesthetic. Most will veer toward a certain style, and it should sync with you.

Set Up On-Site Interviews

You're not just looking for a landscape architect or designer whose work you love; you're looking for someone you can trust. Winnow your list down to two or three and interview them in person. Meet them at the site so they can see your property, and so you can gauge their interest as you describe your ideas and goals. You'll also get a good read on their communication style. The design process is supposed to be collaborative; make sure they listen to your priorities and ask you questions, too.

This is also a good time to share the not-to-exceed number in your budget. They might be able to confirm whether your budget is realistic. If you get the sense that

the job is too small for them, or they're too busy, move on; you want to find someone as fully invested as you.

Get References and Visit a Project

Ask the candidates you're most interested in hiring for references from previous clients, and call them. It's also important to visit at least one of the contractor's completed projects.

Ask for a Proposal

The proposal (which typically also includes the contract for you to review) should outline the scope of work in detail. Expect to find out about all associated costs and fees, who is responsible for what, a timeline for completion of each phase, how change orders will be handled, and a schedule of estimated payments. If you're on the fence between two different designers, it's fine to ask for a proposal from both before making a decision.

Sign a Contract

After you've decided whom to hire, iron out any issues you have with the terms and services detailed in the contract, which should state that the work is to be performed to your specifications and for the bid provided. The more specifics the better: spell out the scope of the work to be done and describe materials (if the project includes a bluestone patio, for instance, specify the dimensions of the pavers to be used). Include a clause stating that the site will be kept clean and the work performed in a timely manner. Insert a clause for inadequate work, stating that it will be repaired to the agreed specifications or allowing you to deduct the cost of repairs from what the contractor is owed. Sign the contract before any work begins.

THE DESIGN MEETING

After a contract has been signed, you'll give your landscape architect or designer a clear and thorough description of your ideas and goals. You'll want to convey how you plan to live in your outdoor spaces; what activities you'll do there; how you want the spaces to appear (e.g., ordered, informal, natural, or a combination); what your favorite colors are; what you like and don't like about your existing landscape; your desired level of maintenance; and, last but not least, your budget. The more information you give up front, the better. Remember, this is a dialogue. Be open to the designer's ideas. That's why you hired him or her.

Site Analysis
The design team will do a thorough site analysis, including measurements and photos; light and wind patterns; the architecture and interior spaces of the house (to see what might be applicable to the outdoor spaces); the neighboring properties (for privacy and noise issues and to see how your site fits into the bigger picture); soil testing; drainage issues; and existing plants and materials (to consider what can be reused in the new design). They'll use this information to make base drawings of the existing landscape.

Schematic Design
Your landscape architect or designer will likely come back with several design options. Typically, these will be color drawings that show the location of all the hardscape features and planting areas, and present ideas for building and plant materials. Take the drawings and spend some time mulling them over. Imagine using the spaces and moving through them. Call the designer if you have questions. When you're ready, offer clear and concise feedback. If there are things you want to change, this is the time.

Construction Drawings and Approvals
Changes based on your feedback will be incorporated in the final construction drawings to obtain bids from landscape contractors. The designer also will coordinate the process of getting any necessary drawings from outside consultants, such as structural, soil, civil engineering, lighting, or irrigation, and submit them for building permits or approvals.

Selecting a Landscape Contractor
After you have a good, detailed set of drawings, bid them out to at least three contractors to get the best price in terms of cost and quality. Weigh the bids against the contractor's reputation. Your landscape architect or designer will likely recommend contractors, and unless you have someone else in mind whom you've vetted, it's a good idea to heed his or her advice. If you can assemble a team that has already been together on a project, you can be relatively sure that they have a good working relationship. That should minimize the amount of supervision (and ensuing hourly fees) required by the design team during the construction phase.

Site Work and Construction
Remember how much fun it used to be to play in the mud? Take a deep breath when your dog tracks dirt through every room in the house, and don't forget to exhale. If you live in a row house and everything needs to go through the front door, make sure the contractor puts a premium on protecting the interior.

Installation
Finally. Landscape architects and designers typically oversee placement of plant materials by the contractor. One difference from an interior remodel is that in a newly installed garden, plants may look skimpy. But don't be disappointed with these small versions of their future selves. Plants will mature soon enough to fill the empty spaces.

EIGHT WAYS TO KEEP YOUR SANITY (AND BE A GOOD CLIENT) ALONG THE WAY

❶ Open the lines of communication early.

Start the process by clearly expressing your goals and ideas so your design team knows exactly what you want and can work them into the final drawings.

❷ Tune out unsolicited advice.

Friends included. Everyone has a different dream. You've thought long and hard about yours; stick to it.

❸ Work with, not against, the seasons.

Limit weather delays as much as possible by timing your project so the design phase is completed in the off season, and building and installation happen within the spring-to-fall window.

❹ Work out a schedule.

Ask for a detailed schedule outlining what will happen when, during each phase of the project, so you know what to expect from week to week.

❺ Remember your neighbors.

To avoid the stress of unhappy next-door neighbors, let them know in advance if there will be time periods when the construction process will be particularly noisy or disruptive: jackhammers, tree removal, trucks, or debris boxes clogging the street.

❻ Trust your design team.

After you have a master plan, step back and let the professionals do their job. Keep the communication lines open, but don't tie up the team with indecision or the need for unnecessary handholding.

❼ Take the long view.

Keep your eye on the vision you're working toward, the dangling carrot. This is where having a master plan comes in handy. Use it to stay focused on the big picture. When you're dealing with Mother Nature, sometimes bad weather can have a drastic effect on the schedule, holding up work and even impacting the arrival of plants in the nursery.

❽ Pay your bills on time.

You've signed contracts stating when payment is expected for different phases of the project. Respect the due dates unless someone isn't doing the job. Delaying payment will frustrate your design team and contractor, and potentially stop work on the project.

———————

PRO TIP

Lost and Found

"Found objects give an outdoor space a lot of character and tell a story. We like to use recycled steel and aluminum for plant containers or walls. If you have a rocky site, harvest the stone and use it to build retaining walls."

—ERIC BLASEN, landscape architect,
Blasen Landscape Architecture

The Process

Expert Advice

06

The Punch List

Unless you're going it alone with a landscape contractor, a big part of your design team's job is to visit the site regularly to make sure the contractor is following the design and installation specifications in their drawings. Many punch list items need to be checked along the way, before everything is veiled under a layer of mulch.

EIGHT THINGS TO CHECK BEFORE THE FINAL RUN-THROUGH

❶ Tweak the lighting.
Have your landscape architect or designer come back at night to see if the lighting needs to be fine-tuned. Too much light is as bad as not enough.

❷ Test the irrigation system.
Make sure the plants are getting water, the sprinklers aren't overspraying, and there are no drainage or puddle issues. Ask the landscape contractor for a map of your irrigation zones and a lesson on how to operate the controls.

❸ Get a plant list.
Ask your landscape architect or designer for a planting map with the names and locations of all the plants, as well as care information for them. Even if you're not planning to do the maintenance yourself, it will come in handy if your gardener has questions.

❹ Gather product information.
Assemble a binder to hold all your warranties, product manuals, and care information for furniture, barbecue equipment, lighting, irrigation, and tools.

❺ Buy furniture covers.
If you didn't purchase them with the furniture, do it before bad weather starts. Teak furniture can withstand the elements, but if you live in a climate with a lot of rain, teak will hold up even better with a little protection. Designate a dry place in the garage or garden shed for storing cushions, umbrellas, and the like in bad weather.

❻ Set up ongoing maintenance.
Creating a garden is a little like having a baby: after your new family member arrives, you have to start taking care of it. Many landscape architects or designers and contractors offer ongoing maintenance services after the project is finished. If you were planning to hire help, consider using them: they now know your garden better than anyone. Otherwise, ask them to meet with the gardener you hire to pass along plant care information.

❼ Thank everyone who worked on the job.
They deserve to know how much you appreciate their help. If you're lucky—knock on wood—there won't be any problems you need them to fix. But if you end the project on good terms, you'll feel more comfortable e-mailing or calling them with any small questions that come up.

❽ Make sure plants are thriving.
Continue to monitor plant health and let your design team or landscape contractor know if any plants aren't doing well. They can recheck the soil and help adjust the irrigation if need be.

PRO TIP

Care and Feeding

"The physical work of garden maintenance is therapeutic and soothing in so many ways. Concentrating on the task at hand makes other worries slip away—watching what flowers, what's ready to harvest. Even weeding can be relaxing."

—SILVINA BLASEN, landscape designer,
Blasen Landscape Architecture

Resources We Swear By

ANTIQUES AND VINTAGE

Big Daddy's

Los Angeles and San Francisco, CA
bdantiques.com
Prop stylists' and designers' go-to source for early American, European, and Asian garden ornaments and vintage furniture. And big is right: the LA location fills a former soundstage.

Circa50

Manchester Center, VT
circa50.com
Specializing in midcentury modern designs, this shop is a go-to resource for the butterfly chair (designed in 1938 by Jorge Ferrari-Hardoy).

Circa Antiques

Westport, CT
circaantiques.com
One-of-a-kind urns, pots, and planters imported from Europe.

eBay

ebay.com
Yes, it's still possible to get deals on the world's biggest auction site. Two tricks—shop locally (so you can pick up bulky purchases and avoid shipping costs) *and* use advanced searches to shop internationally (source a design from the country where it was made and you'll likely pay less, offsetting the cost of shipping).

1stdibs

1stdibs.com
A collective representing top antiques dealers of every specialty from around the world.

Jamb

London, England
jamb.co.uk
Classic garden urns, orbs, busts, fountains, vases, and sphinxes are hand-carved from solid blocks of antique statuary marble and stone, based on historic designs chosen by owners Will Fisher and Charlotte Freemantle.

Obsolete

Venice, CA
obsoleteinc.com
This LA-based antiques purveyor stocks garden sculpture and curiosities for classical landscapes. The owner travels to Europe every month and returns with French metal window boxes, nineteenth-century wooden grape bins, and rewired verdigris copper garden lanterns.

Olde Good Things

Los Angeles, CA; New York, NY, and Scranton, PA
ogtstore.com
With three locations, Olde Good Things sells salvaged architectural elements such as iron gates and fences as well as a range of antique garden statues, fountains, and patio furniture.

Wyeth

New York City and Sagaponack, NY
wyeth.nyc
"Own the original" is a compelling reason to source outdoor lighting from this best-of-breed antiques dealer, which specializes in early twentieth-century industrial-style sconces, marine lighting, and commercial-grade fixtures.

APPLIANCES

Note that some high-end brands, such as Wolf, KitchenAid, and GE Monogram, are not available for online purchase if you live more than a specified number of miles from a seller's location. Refer to each manufacturer's website to find the nearest vendors.

Abt Electronics

abt.com
The go-to source for outfitting an outdoor dining space, Abt has everything from barbecue grills to outdoor heaters to dining accessories to weather-resistant outdoor speakers.

AJ Madison

Brooklyn, NY
ajmadison.com
All the appliances you need to create a full-service outdoor kitchen, including grills, bars, refrigerators, and patio heaters.

Plessers Appliance

Babylon, NY
plessers.com
Retailer of classic outdoor kitchen appliance brands such as Viking, Weber, Wolf, and KitchenAid.

US Appliance

us-appliance.com
High-end electronics and appliances, including a large selection of grills.

ARCHITECTURAL SALVAGE

Madeira Furniture

Van Nuys, CA (by appointment)
madeirafurniture.net
Reclaimed lumber specialists focusing on rare woods from Brazil.

Ohmega Salvage

Berkeley, CA
ohmegasalvage.com
Think high-end junkyard: architectural elements and hardscape materials removed from Bay Area buildings find a second life on the grounds of a sprawling Berkeley salvage yard.

Retrouvius

London, England
retrouvius.com
London's premier salvage showroom is run by a husband-and-wife team of celebrated interior designers.

Urban Archaeology

Boston, MA; Bridgehampton and New York, NY; and Chicago, IL
urbanarchaeology.com
Estate-quality metal details, at prices you pay for the patina of age.

Urban Remains

Chicago, IL
urbanremainschicago.com
A mecca of reclaimed artifacts and oddities from urban commercial, residential, and industrial buildings.

DECORATIVE ACCESSORIES

ABC Carpet and Home

Delray Beach, FL; Bronx and New York, NY
abchome.com
What started as New York's premier source for rugs has expanded into an indoor souk offering everything for the home, including terra-cotta pots from Belgium, outdoor dining tables, and one-of-a-kind vintage garden benches.

Badia Design

Los Angeles, CA
badiadesign.com
High-quality stamped metal Moroccan lanterns, imported since the 1990s, lend a Moorish air to both classic and contemporary gardens.

Ben Pentreath Ltd.

London, England
benpentreath.com
London architect and interior designer Ben Pentreath has a shop in Bloomsbury where he sells vintage and new housewares and accessories, from candlesticks to seashells.

Ben Wolff Pottery

New Preston, CT
benwolffpottery.com
Son of the well-known potter Guy Wolff, Ben sells a range of handmade ceramic pots in classic shapes and subtle, hard-to-find colors, including black, gray, and buff.

Burford Garden Company

Cotswolds, England
burford.co.uk
Four generations ago, family-run Burford Garden Company (and plant nursery) began selling an eclectic collection of outdoor furniture, picnic ware, outdoor lighting, and plants and seeds.

Dash & Albert

Pittsfield, MA
dashandalbert.annieselke.com
Designers of outdoor rugs that deserve a spot inside as well, this manufacturer has cracked the code on how to create weather-resistant textiles without sacrificing style.

Dunlin

dunlin.com.au
A curated collection of high-quality lighting fixtures and accessories, including barn sconces, carriage lanterns, and handblown glass terrariums.

Etsy

etsy.com
This site is a gardeners' upscale flea market: a universe of handmade, DIY garden accessories and outdoor furniture, both vintage and new, ranging from macramé planters to stylish birdhouses.

Ferm Living

fermliving.com
This Danish design studio makes concrete pots, stoneware hanging planters, and modernist wire trellises.

Finnish Design Shop

finnishdesignshop.com
A source of Scandinavian imports from designers such as Eva Solo, Jasper Morrison, and Normann Copenhagen.

The Gardener

Berkeley and Healdsburg, CA
thegardener.com
With its selection of handmade wooden bowls, hand-dyed textiles, and exotic rare orchids, this Northern California garden store is selling a lifestyle as much as accessories.

Garden Trading

Oxfordshire, England
gardentrading.co.uk
Quietly tasteful garden necessities including pathway lights, workbenches, and tin watering cans.

Greenhouse & Co.

Brooklyn, NY
greenhouseandcompany.com
Purveyors of eco-friendly wares for Brooklynites and kindred spirits.

Gump's

San Francisco, CA
gumps.com
A venerable doyenne of the San Francisco retail scene, offering ceramic garden stools, vases, and weather-safe botanical throw pillows. Since 1861 it's been a showcase of the sorts of exotic and luxurious furnishings that California gold rush millionaires exulted in.

Jaques of London

London, England
jaqueslondon.co.uk
The Jaques family has been manufacturing handmade wooden croquet sets since the 1800s, when John Jaques II won a gold medal (still in the family's possession) for introducing croquet at the Great Exhibition of 1851.

Jayson Home
Chicago, IL
jaysonhome.com
An emporium of modern and vintage furniture and accessories with an emphasis on solid midwestern comfort.

John Derian
New York, NY, and Provincetown, MA
johnderian.com
An artist and antiques dealer, Derian has a keen eye for discovering new artists and beautiful textiles. His eponymous Manhattan shop sells the work of artist Hugo Guinness, Astier de Villatte ceramics, and Moroccan poufs.

L'Aviva Home
New York, NY (by appointment)
lavivahome.com
A laid-back look can be achieved with Laura Aviva's collection of Moroccan pom-pom blankets, Bolivian hammocks, and hand-woven Belgian linen pillows.

Lekker Home
Boston, MA
lekkerhome.com
Furniture, rugs, and pathway torches with a Dutch and Scandinavian aesthetic.

Les Potagers de Thomas
lespotagersdethomas.be
Classic, elevated planter boxes fitted with wrought-iron and glass conservatories, manufactured by a husband-and-wife team in Belgium to raise funds for their son, Thomas, who has learning disabilities.

March
San Francisco, CA
marchsf.com
Tastemaker Sam Hamilton's housewares and garden and kitchen accessories store offers a meticulously curated collection of Belgian planters, outdoor furniture, picnic and dining accessories, and hurricane candle lanterns.

Matter
New York, NY
mattermatters.com
A gallery that, since 2003, has showcased internationally sourced designs that are as much art as object. Outdoor offerings include a configurable hardwood fort and Jasper Morrison lounge chairs.

Merci
Paris, France
merci-merci.com
Housed in a former wallpaper factory in the heart of the Marais district in Paris, Merci brings together the best of vintage and contemporary, costly and affordable garden pots and vases.

Mini Farm Box
Los Angeles, CA
minifarmbox.com
To maximize growing space, designer Conor Fitzpatrick devised a collection of raised beds made from FSC-certified cedar. Stackable and termite- and rot-resistant, they come in a variety of sizes.

MQuan Studio Designs
New York, NY
mquan.com
Ceramicist Michele Quan's iconic jingle bell garlands on twisted rope have defined a new silhouette for hanging sculpture for the garden (and spawned many imitations).

NK Shop
Los Angeles, CA
nickeykehoe.com
Planters, birdhouses, watering cans, and doormats with a distinctly Southern California vibe (think boho-LA rainforest), from interior designers Todd Nickey and Amy Kehoe.

Pawleys Island Hammocks
Greenville, NC
pawleysislandhammocks.com
Founded in 1889 by South Carolina riverboat captain Joshua John "Cap'n Josh" Ward, Pawleys Island Hammocks remains (125 years later) the gold standard.

Paxton Gate
Portland, OR, and San Francisco, CA
paxtongate.com
Skulls and taxidermy mixed in with air plants, terrariums, and Japanese gardening tools.

RE
Cambridge and London, England
re-foundobjects.com
Secondhand, vintage, and new products (many designed by Jenny Vaughan and Simon Young) give this emporium the feel of an old-fashioned tag sale. You never know what you'll find, from a rusted porch glider to moss-covered plant pots.

Seibert & Rice
Short Hills, NJ
seibert-rice.com
Imported from the mecca of terra-cotta in Impruneta, Italy, this shop's selection of planters and urns in a wide range of styles and sizes are handmade, frost-proof, and likely to last a lifetime.

Sprout Home
Brooklyn, NY, and Chicago, IL
sprouthome.com
A large selection of planters and terrariums, as well as a small but stylish collection of outdoor furniture.

Summer House
Mill Valley, CA
summerhouse57millvalley.com
Owners Jane Walter and Robert Adams have an eye for ahead-of-the-curve accessories and furnishings, with one-of-a-kind vintage finds and a collection of over-dyed rugs.

Terrain
Glen Mills, PA, and Westport, CT
shopterrain.com
Founded in 2008, this upscale version of a local garden center sells furnishings and accessories ranging from teak lounge chairs to terrariums and tools.

Toast
London, England
toa.st/us
A constantly evolving collection of artfully practical products for outdoor living. In a given season, the offerings may include portable barbecue grills, books about cloud pruning, and storm lanterns in a rainbow of colors.

Variopinte
Barcelona, Spain
variopinte.com
Italian designer Stefania di Petrillo creates old-fashioned enamelware in modern designs and colors. Her Variopinte line includes dishwasher-safe cutlery, plates, and bowls.

Zinc Details
San Francisco, CA
zincdetails.com
Modern furniture and exterior accessories range from stainless-steel house numbers to doorbells to Acapulco chairs.

FABRICS AND CUSHIONS

Ian Mankin

London, England
ianmankin.co.uk
The British patriarch of ticking, Ian Mankin stocks a wide range of striped (as well as natural) cotton, linen, and oilcloth fabrics.

Lake August

Los Angeles, CA
lakeaugust.com
Inspired by her mother's and grandmother's Southern California gardens, designer Alexis Hartman created a collection of botanical print fabrics handprinted on Belgian linen.

Les Toiles du Soleil

New York, NY
lestoilesdusoleilnyc.com
Classic French Catalan striped fabrics and goods made from them, including wooden deck chairs with sling seats.

Liberty of London

London, England
liberty.co.uk
Beyond the trademark floral fabrics, tucked away on an upper floor of this venerable landmark department store you'll find a selection of birdhouses, garden trowels, and gardening gloves.

Sunbrella

sunbrella.com
Manufacturer of outdoor fabrics for awnings, canopies, outdoor furniture, pillows, and curtains.

Virginia Johnson

Toronto, Canada
virginiajohnson.com
Turning her attention to fanciful botanically inspired patterns, textile designer and illustrator Virginia Johnson designs throws, pillows, and colorful ceramic garden stools.

Zangra

zangra.com
A Belgian upstart devoted to selling "well-sourced bits and pieces" (of its own design and by others) offers an eclectic collection that includes bee houses, doormats, and driveway pavers.

FURNITURE

A + R Store

aplusrstore.com
Modern pop art and designs from around the globe.

Alias

Bergamo, Italy
alias.design
Since 1979, this shop has combined minimalism and an Italian design sensibility; outdoor furnishings include bar carts, lounge chairs, dining tables, and upholstered sofas with cushions impervious to the weather.

AllModern

allmodern.com
An online department store of contemporary design: conversation pit seating, outdoor dining tables and chairs, and sturdy shade umbrellas.

Another Country

anothercountry.com
Clear and elegant reinterpretations of farmhouse furniture are handmade in England of solid oak and other sustainable woods; for outdoors, the range includes trestle tables, benches, and wooden house numbers.

Brown Jordan

brownjordan.com
Brown Jordan has been manufacturing high-quality furniture and furnishings (including sturdy garden umbrellas) since 1945 in a wide range of styles, from traditional to contemporary.

Casamidy

Brussels, Belgium (by appointment), and San Miguel de Allende, Mexico
casamidy.com
Known for its incredible outdoor lanterns, this San Miguel–based design studio also makes opulent metal-framed furniture and accessories handcrafted by local artisans.

The Conran Shop

London, England
conranshop.co.uk
The standard-bearer of functional, well-made, and eye-opening contemporary design.

Curran Home

Seattle, Washington
curranonline.com
For twenty years, a reliable U.S. source of high-end furniture from overseas, including the collections from Skagerak, Royal Botania, Skargaarden, and Barlow Tyrie.

Design Public

designpublic.com
A virtual emporium of modernist wares, from Kartell stools to Scandinavian loungers.

Fermob

Thoissey, France
fermob.com
French manufacturer of the definitive café furniture, including bistro tables for two, metal folding chairs, and benches available in a staggering range of colors.

Fjørn

Carmel by the Sea, CA
fjorn.com
Online retailer with a brick-and-mortar shop devoted to Nordic designs, including steamer deck loungers, teak tables, and stacking chairs.

The Future Perfect

Brooklyn and New York, NY, and San Francisco, CA
thefutureperfect.com
At the vanguard of contemporary style, Future Perfect was the first U.S. store to carry Piet Hein Eek's teak tables, benches, and chairs.

George Smith

Chicago, IL; Los Angeles, CA; and New York, NY
georgesmith.com
The last word in tufting; this designer of pricey upholstered classics made in England offers outdoor furnishings capable of withstanding the elements anywhere from "super-yachts to your own private oasis."

Horne

shophorne.com
Horne's selection to "bring a bit of sophistication to your personal swath of the rugged outdoors" includes modern teak dining tables and midcentury planters.

Janus et Cie

Los Angeles, CA (with showrooms worldwide)
janusetcie.com

Launched in the 1970s by designer Janice Feldman, Janus et Cie offers high-quality outdoor furniture with clean, modern lines in materials from wicker to aluminum wire to weather-resistant hardwood.

Jardinique

Hampshire, England
jardinique.com

Classically inspired, climate-tested outdoor furniture including the iconic Westport chair, the original from which all Adirondack chairs are descended.

Koskela

Sydney, Australia
koskela.com.au

This furniture design company with an expansive Sydney showroom is a must-see for Australian modern design.

Loll Designs

Duluth, MN
lolldesigns.com

Loll's modern outdoor furniture, planter boxes, and garden accessories are manufactured in the United States of recycled plastic.

Mjölk

Toronto, Canada
mjolk.ca

A tastemaker couple's boutique of Scandinavian and Japanese design (and often an inspired convergence of the two) carries the perfect garden bench, designed by Jasper Morrison for his own use.

Munder-Skiles

Garrison, NY, and Los Angeles, CA
munder-skiles.com

Beautifully proportioned, graceful garden and outdoor furniture is made to order and meant to last forever.

Piet Hein Eek

Eindhoven, Netherlands
pietheineek.nl/en

Dutch designer Piet Hein Eek's weighty and dramatic furnishings, including garden benches, chairs, and dining tables made of recycled teak, are one-of-a-kind pieces constructed in a factory adjacent to his studio.

Rose Tarlow Melrose House

Los Angeles, CA, and New York, NY
rosetarlow.com

The glam interior designer and antiquarian produces her own furniture, wallpaper, and textiles, including outdoor fabrics in ticking stripes, neutral solid colors, and subtle floral patterns.

Scandinavian Grace

Shokan, NY
scandinaviangrace.com

Brooklyn retail veteran Fredrik Larsson decamped to the Catskills to open a 4,500-square-foot shop carrying a wide range of Scandinavian goods, including campbeds, camping chairs, oil lamps, and tea light holders.

Skandium

London, England (three locations)
skandium.com

A source for Bertoia wire side chairs and round Saarinen tables, Skandium has two London shops, an outpost at Selfridges, and a well-developed online store.

Skargaarden

Gävle, Sweden
skargaarden.com

From its headquarters near the Arctic Circle, this Scandinavian manufacturer of high-quality outdoor furnishings produces "furniture for these precious moments; for the short Swedish summers. We can't compromise because every second counts."

Y Living

yliving.com

Design Within Reach's larger (and less rigorously curated) online competitor carries upholstered outdoor sofas, bar carts, benches, and a wide range of outdoor accessories.

GREENHOUSES AND CONSERVATORIES

Hartley Botanic

Manchester, England
hartley-botanic.com

These made-to-measure greenhouses have been manufactured in the UK since 1938, "engineered to cope with the severest storms."

Serres d'Antan

Savigny-sur-Braye, France
serresdantan.com

Makers of bespoke steel and glass greenhouses, conservatories, and doors for moats.

SturdiBuilt

Portland, OR
sturdi-built.com

Redwood and glass greenhouse kits from a small, family-run business.

HARDSCAPE MATERIALS

Ann Sacks

Locations nationwide
annsacks.com

A leading national source for modern surface materials such as concrete, stone, and mosaic tiles.

Carocim

Aix-en-Provence, France
carocim.com

This Provençal company has been making patterned and solid-colored encaustic cement tiles since 1850.

EverLawn

Poulton-le-Fylde, England
everlawn.co.uk

Synthetic grass woven with high-quality, soft yarns to simulate the look and feel of live turf grass.

Fireclay Tile

San Francisco and San Jose, CA
fireclaytile.com

Handmade in California, the tile selection includes products for roofs, pools, hearths, and staircases.

ForeverLawn

North Canton, OH
foreverlawn.com

An architect's favorite, this high-quality artificial lawn from DuPont is made with a layer of recycled plastic.

Granada Tile

Los Angeles, CA
granadatile.com

The company derives its name and inspiration from the historic city of Granada in Nicaragua, where tiles are manufactured using a centuries-old process: pigmented cement is poured into intricate metal molds, then pressed and left to air-dry.

Grass Concrete

Yorkshire, England
Grasscrete.com
Since 1970, makers of green roof
materials and permeable concrete
pavers.

Kismet Tile

kismettile.com
Concrete tile in modern geometric
patterns fabricated in Morocco.

Popham Design

pophamdesign.com
Popham Design employs Moroccan
artisans to hand-make cement tiles
in an array of designs and colors that
combine traditional elements with a
contemporary twist. Almond trees,
arches, and donkey cart wheels are all
sources of inspiration.

Stone Source

Locations nationwide
stonesource.com
Stone slabs and tiles (both natural and
engineered) as well as ceramic tile.

Vermont Quarries

Mendon, VT
vermontquarries.com
Fabricator of U.S.-quarried white
marble slabs and tiles.

HARDWARE AND HOUSE NUMBERS

Baldwin Hardware

baldwinhardware.com
Maker of high-quality door hardware
since 1946.

Bouvet

bouvet.com
Doorbells, gate latches, door
hardware, hinges, and hooks hand-
forged in France since 1884.

Crown City Hardware

Pasadena, CA
restoration.com
Crown City has been offering a range
of hardware for windows, doors, and
screens since opening its doors (as
Thompson's Hardware) in 1916.

E. R. Butler & Co.

Boston, MA; Milan, Italy, and New York, NY
(by appointment)
erbutler.com
The country's most refined custom
hardware manufacturer specializes in
early American, Federal, and Georgian
fixtures for doors, windows, and gates.

Heath Ceramics

Los Angeles, San Francisco (two locations),
and Sausalito, CA
heathceramics.com
Tile house numbers in architect
Richard Neutra's elegant midcentury
font (in addition to a vast line of
handmade tiles in both glazed and
matte finishes). Pro user tip: visit
the "seconds" factory showroom in
Sausalito for fabulous finds.

House of Antique Hardware

Portland, OR
houseofantiquehardware.com
Hardware for window sashes and
casements, door sets, kick plates, and
bronze or brass mail slots are among
the reproduction American designs.

Merit Hardware

Washington, PA
meritmetal.com
Since 1876, makers of simple brass
hardware, from screen-door knobs to
floor registers.

Ramsign

ramsign.com
Dutch purveyor since 1991 of enameled
porcelain house numbers and address
signs.

HOSES AND IRRIGATION

Dripworks

Willits, CA
dripworks.com
One-stop shopping for drip-irrigation
supplies and water-conserving kits.

Rain Bird

Azusa, CA
rainbird.com
Everything you need for a water-saving
system; from sprinklers, timers, valves,
and micro sprays to drip water kits.

Water Right

McMinnville, OR
waterrightinc.com
This family-owned company makes
toxin-free garden hoses that won't kink.

LIGHTING

Aldo Bernardi

aldobernardi.com
Hand-finished ceramic porch fixtures
and outdoor wall lights from a factory
on the outskirts of Venice.

Barn Light Electric

Titusville, FL
barnlightelectric.com
Since 2008, founders Bryan and
Donna Scott have been on a mission
to bring back high-quality American
industrial lighting.

Bega

Menden, Germany, and Santa Barbara, CA
bega.com
German precision, manufactured in
America: pathway lights, spotlights,
downlights, and wall sconces.

Circa Lighting

Savannah, GA, and locations nationwide
circalighting.com
Traditional and classic fixtures,
including porch lights and outdoor
sconces by designers E. F. Chapman,
Barbara Barry, and Thomas O'Brien.

Lumens

Sacramento, CA
lumens.com
A lighting emporium with a modernist
bent that offers bollards, torches, and
spotlights for paths, decks, and ponds.

Rejuvenation

Berkeley and Los Angeles, CA; Portland,
OR; and Seattle, WA
rejuvenation.com
Rejuvenation carries reproduction
lighting, doorbells, house numbers,
and other exterior hardware in styles
from colonial to midcentury modern.

Roger Pradier

Saint-Maur-des-Fossés, France
roger-pradier.com
Since 1910, a French lantern maker with
a high-quality collection of lighting for
lampposts, pathways, and exterior walls.

Schoolhouse Electric & Supply Co.

New York, NY, and Portland, OR
schoolhouseelectric.com
Industrial- and vintage-style lighting
parts of all sorts (including lightbulbs)
and a modern factory sconce for
outdoor use.

Y Lighting

ylighting.com

The giant inventory of modern and contemporary lighting includes pathway lighting, LED designs, and outdoor ceiling fans.

NATIONAL STORES

Ace Hardware

acehardware.com

An easy first stop for staples (think galvanized buckets and painters' drop cloths). Thanks to the fact that every Ace is independently owned, the chain has a neighborly vibe.

CB2

cb2.com

Crate & Barrel's youthful spinoff offers well-priced outdoor furniture and accessories.

Crate & Barrel

crateandbarrel.com

Founded in Chicago in the 1960s to introduce no-nonsense European design to America, the chain holds true to its origins with teak furniture, weather-resistant cushions, and sturdy zinc balcony planters.

Design Within Reach

dwr.com

DWR helped kick off the midcentury design revival by making Bertoia, Tolix, and Knoll classics accessible and relevant to the way we live today.

Home Depot

homedepot.com

The big-box convenience store for inexpensive tools, building materials, paint, and more.

IKEA

ikea.com

Scandinavian design—from outdoor sectionals to charcoal grills and deck flooring—priced for all.

Lowe's

lowes.com

Home Depot's competitor is especially handy for DIY projects, with inexpensive materials such as lumber and wire fencing.

Restoration Hardware

restorationhardware.com

Well-made outsized furniture for outdoors, often modeled after Belgian or rustic French designs.

Room & Board

roomandboard.com

Based in Minneapolis, the chain specializes in sturdy modernist furniture.

Sur La Table

surlatable.com

In addition to a broad selection of outdoor dining accessories and tools for grilling, the chain offers tabletop topiaries of rosemary and olive trees.

West Elm

westelm.com

Affordable, modernist design with inventory that changes seasonally in rapid response to the latest trends in outdoor rugs, furniture, and accessories.

Williams-Sonoma

williams-sonoma.com

In addition to selling classic tableware and serving pieces, the chain has an Agrarian gardening line offering raised-bed planter kits, chicken coops, and well-made tools.

THE NEW GENERAL STORE

Ancient Industries

ancientindustries.com

Created by "Gardenista 100" author Kendra Wilson in partnership with her sister, Megan, Ancient Industries is an inspired compendium of British and European garden accessories and housewares made the same way for eons.

Atomic Garden

Oakland, CA

atomicgardenoakland.com

Check out this eclectic shop for quirky home goods, from herb choppers and beeswax candles to twine stands and ceremonial incense sticks.

Baileys Home and Garden

Herefordshire, England

baileyshome.com

Sally and Mark Bailey are British design gurus who preach brilliantly about the use of natural materials and mixing up the old, the new, and the reclaimed. Their compound consists of a shop, a café in a barn, workrooms, a smithy, and their own home—which puts in appearances in *Handmade Home* and other books by the Baileys.

Best Made Company

New York, NY

bestmadeco.com

For manly, outdoorsy design junkies: the ultimate handmade axes, first-aid kits, and Pendleton-manufactured red wool blankets. Best Made's cloth-covered extension cord is a classic.

Bitters Co.

Seattle, WA

bittersco.com

Founded in 1993, this family-owned general store offers well-crafted housewares, from coat hooks to colorful doormats, many made from recycled materials and of Bitters's own design.

Brook Farm General Store

Brooklyn, NY

brookfarmgeneralstore.com

Here you'll find an eclectic mix of canvas camp cots, folding teak loungers, and ceramic hanging planters.

Canoe

Portland, OR

canoeonline.net

Wooden birdcalls, bamboo rakes, and leather fly swatters are part of a meticulously edited range of items, many of which hail from Portland.

Everyday Needs

Auckland, New Zealand

everyday-needs.com

A star New Zealand stylist's carefully assembled collection includes copper hand tools, bamboo cloches, and willow garden trugs.

JM Drygoods

Austin, TX

jmdrygoods.com

JM Drygoods stocks Acapulco chairs, hand-embroidered Mexican textiles, and handmade ceramics as well as Silla, JMDG's line of leather, steel, and furniture made in Marfa.

Kaufmann Mercantile

kaufmann-mercantile.com

An online catalog of well-designed goods that come with a story: poplar wood crates (made by Pennsylvania Amish), a tree swing (from reclaimed pine), and U.S.-made cedar patio planters (designed by an organic farming expert).

Kiosk

New York, NY

kioskkiosk.com

A witty curated collection imported from around the world includes a Romanian galvanized pail and a red metal garden tool set from Sweden.

Labour and Wait

London, England

labourandwait.co.uk

Timeless, well-made garden essentials include enameled watering cans and dibber-and-label sets.

Manufactum

Berlin, Düsseldorf, Frankfurt, Hamburg, Köln, Munich, Stuttgart, and Waltorp, Germany

manufactum.com

This trailblazing German site features high-quality, beautifully designed biergarten furniture, freestanding outdoor showers, and garden tools.

Objects of Use

Oxford, England

objectsofuse.com

Serious gardeners will want to put these last-a-lifetime tools on their birthday wish lists: Austrian "scythe sickles," razor hoes (right- and left-handed models), and galvanized adjustable-fan leaf rakes.

Old Faithful Shop

Vancouver, Canada

oldfaithfulshop.com

"Good quality goods for simple, everyday living" include terrariums, twine stands, and a Dutch-style hand broom for a potting table.

Tortoise General Store

Venice, CA

tortoisegeneralstore.com

Florists' scissors, flower frogs, and other ikebana accessories are among the slow-design standouts from Japan.

PAINTS AND STAINS

Benjamin Moore Paints

benjaminmoore.com

Thousands of tried-and-true colors and new rich tones (thanks to technology that mixes up to eight hues per color) are available in exterior formulations suitable for surfaces from stucco to steel; plus, there's a wide range of stains for decks and fences.

Eve Ashcraft

eveashcraft.com

Paint whisperer and Remodelista contributor Eve Ashcraft developed Martha Stewart's first paint lines: Araucana, inspired by hen's eggs, and Everyday Colors. She works as a private palette consultant in New York, but her wisdom is available to all via her book, *The Right Color*, and her line of twenty-eight custom shades for Fine Paints of Europe.

Farrow & Ball

farrow-ball.com

The UK company synonymous with nuanced colors mixed from long-standing formulations and natural ingredients (that are low and zero VOC), Farrow & Ball offers finishes for exterior surfaces. When people ask paint stores to copy Farrow & Ball colors, the results rarely come close.

Fine Paints of Europe

finepaintsofeurope.com

This manufacturer of exterior and interior paints sells a Dutch Door Kit, which supplies premium paint plus all the materials—from sandpaper to primer—for painting an entryway.

Martin Senour Paints

martinsenour.com

You'll find porch floor enamels, wood stains, and formulations for exterior wood, stucco, and metal surfaces from this maker of subtle, layered, and timeless hues since 1878.

Paint Library

London, England

paintandpaperlibrary.com

Colorist David Oliver has a line of historical, traditional, and contemporary hues.

Pratt & Lambert Paints

prattandlambert.com

In business since 1849, Pratt & Lambert sells house and trim paint as well as stains for siding, fences, and decks.

Sydney Harbour Paint Company

shpcompany.com

Australian Peter Lewis was inspired to start his business after discovering formulas for Mediterranean paint washes in his grandfather's archives. The company has a range of water-based finishes, from milk paint to mineral paint to lime wash.

PLANTS AND SEEDS

Annie's Annuals

Richmond, CA

anniesannuals.com

Two and a half acres of plants grown outdoors in 4-inch pots are hardened off and ready for your garden's climate by the time they're sold; owner Annie Hayes specializes in natives, wildflowers, and hard-to-find cultivars.

Baker Creek Heirloom Seeds

Mansfield, MO, and Petaluma, CA

rareseeds.com

Started as a mail-order seed catalog in 1998 by seventeen-year-old Jere Gettle, Baker Creek now has an extensive collection that includes such unusual varieties as Georgia Rattlesnake Watermelon, Dixie Speckled Butterpea Lima Beans, and Gelber Englischer Custard Squash.

Berkeley Horticultural Nursery

Berkeley, CA

berkeleyhort.com

Northern California gardeners make pilgrimages to this family-owned East Bay nursery for a comprehensive selection of native plants, organic seeds, fruit trees, and old roses.

Bonsai Outlet

Fitchburg, MA

bonsaioutlet.com

Bonsai trees, pots, tools, and supplies from owner Ashley Carrier, a hobbyist turned entrepreneur after his wife gave him a bonsai tree for his birthday.

Cottage Gardens

Petaluma, CA

cottagegardensofpet.com

A go-to Bay Area source for high-quality plants, structures (trellises and arbors), pots, and garden ornaments.

David Austin Roses

Albrighton, England

davidaustinroses.com

The last word in commercially grown roses and the first place to look when purchasing. Since founding the company in 1969, rosarian David Austin has introduced 190 cultivars (specializing in breeding repeat bloomers with the fragrance and appearance of old roses).

Ernst Seeds

Meadville, PA

ernstseed.com

A proponent of restoring natural landscapes, this family-owned company offers more than four hundred species of native and naturalized seeds.

Flora Grubb Gardens

San Francisco, CA

floragrubb.com

One of our favorite greenery experts, the aptly named Flora Grubb is an indie landscape designer who helped pioneer the use of air plants in urban settings and vertical succulent gardens (she sells DIY kits). Her Bayview shop doubles as a coffee bar.

Green Jeans Garden Supply

Mill Valley, CA

greenjeansgardensupply.com

From house blends of organic fertilizers to pots and planters from local artisans, owners (and husband-and-wife team) Kevin Sadlier and Xander Wessells offer a wide range of accessories, native plants, and houseplants.

High Mowing Seeds

Wolcott, VT

highmowingseeds.com

High Mowing was the first organic seed company to verify that its six-hundred-plus varieties are non-GMO. Many of its vegetable, herb, flower, and cover crop seeds are grown on its forty-acre farm.

Hudson Valley Seed Company

Accord, NY

seedlibrary.org

Founded by a librarian who started adding seeds to the catalog for patrons to "borrow," the small upstate company now sells its own varieties of heirloom vegetable, herb, and flower seeds as well as seeds from local farmers.

Inner Gardens

Culver City, LA

innergardens.com

Landscape designers' go-to source for specimen-size trees and plants, special succulents, and orchids.

John Scheepers Kitchen Garden Seeds

Bantam, CT

kitchengardenseeds.com

From salsify to Rat Tail radishes, an eclectic collection of seeds (including vegetables, fruits, flowers, and herbs) from a company founded by Dutchman John Theodore Scheepers after he came to America in 1897.

Lambley Nursery

Victoria, Australia

lambley.com.au

Drought-tolerant, frost-hardy plants from around the world grow in owner David Glenn's sprawling garden beds.

Old House Gardens

Ann Arbor, MI

oldhousegardens.com

Owner Scott Kunst has an uncanny ability to unearth the rare, the antique, and the charming; his collection of heirloom flower bulbs is unparalleled. We look forward every autumn to his unusual varieties of broken tulips (responsible for the seventeenth-century Holland tulip craze).

Real Ornamentals

realornamentals.com

Specializing in palms and tropical plants, this online houseplant store ships to forty-eight states.

Renee's Seeds

Felton, CA

reneesgarden.com

Heirloom, certified organic, and open-pollinated seeds are tested for every U.S. growing zone.

Succulent Gardens

Castroville, CA

sgplants.com

Owner Robin Stockwell has been working with succulent plants since 1972 and has a collection of more than four hundred varieties.

The Sill

New York, NY

thesill.com

Created in 2012 as a houseplant delivery service for NYC residents and an online purveyor of easy-care plants and locally made pots, founder Eliza Blank's company has expanded to include a retail shop on Manhattan's Lower East Side (where she also offers plant-sitting services).

Snug Harbor Farm

Kennebunk, ME

snugharborfarm.com

We know people who make the drive to Maine just for an opportunity to stop in at this well-stocked nursery and greenhouse, where the year-round offerings include topiaries grown in hand-thrown terra-cotta pots, planters, and trellises (plus there's a seasonal flower and farm stand).

Territorial Seeds

Cottage Grove, OR

territorialseed.com

This family-owned operation grows and tests many of its seeds on its forty-four acres of trial grounds in the Pacific Northwest. At its nursery and shop, the company also sells garden plants and supplies.

White Flower Farm

Litchfield, CT

whiteflowerfarm.com

Our first stop for high-quality garden plants when we order online, the company still hews to the 1930s philosophy of founders William Harris and Jane Grant in "discarding the fakes and weaklings . . . and propagating the very best."

SHOWERS, SAUNAS, AND SINKS

eFaucets

efaucets.com

In addition to good customer service and user ratings, eFaucets offers one of the largest online selections of outdoor showers and utility sinks.

Quality Bath

qualitybath.com

High-end stainless-steel outdoor kitchen and utility sinks, outdoor shower parts and fixtures, and Japanese soaking tubs for decks.

The Sauna Place

Cookeville, TN
saunaplace.com

From portable saunas to freestanding outbuildings, a wide selection of sauna kits and accessories.

Tectona

Paris, France (and other locations throughout Europe)
tectona.net

High-quality, freestanding showers from a French purveyor of contemporary outdoor furnishings.

Vintage Tub & Bath

vintagetub.com

Freestanding outdoor bathtubs (claw-foot and reproduction styles) and outdoor shower sets.

TOOLS

Burgon & Ball

Sheffield, England
burgonandball.com

Manufacturing tools since 1730, the company offers a wide selection of high-quality, sturdy garden tools that do not compromise on quality, as an endorsement from the Royal Horticultural Society attests.

DeWit Tool Company

Kornhorn, Netherlands
dewittoolsusa.com

Four generations of the deWit family have made handmade tools since 1898. With forged steel blades and FSC-certified wood handles, both long-handled and hand tools live up to the company motto: "More than a tool, it's an heirloom."

Felco Store

felcostore.com

Swiss-made Felco pruners (available with a wide variety of grips and blades, and in left-handed versions) are the go-to choice of most gardeners we know. Replacement parts make it possible to use one pair for life.

Fisher Blacksmithing

Bozeman, MT
fisherblacksmithing.com

Blacksmith Tuli Fisher founded his company after developing a passion for gardening. His hand-forged steel tools with American black walnut handles are as much works of art as friends in the field.

Garrett Wade

New York, NY
garrettwade.com

Garrett Wade has been selling fine tools since 1975. The company's buyers travel the world to assemble a best-of-class selection of garden, woodworking, and workshop tools.

Grafa

grafa.com.au

Australia-based toolmaker Travis Blandford and partner Harriet Devlin offer a stylish collection of sturdy bronze-and-copper hand tools born from recycled lengths of copper plumbing.

Niwaki

niwaki.com

UK-based gardener Jake Hobson founded Niwaki a decade ago to introduce Japan's lightweight tripod ladders and high-quality pruning tools to the rest of the world.

PKS Bronze

Bad Ischl, Austria
kupferspuren.at

The company's beautiful and long-lasting copper gardening tools don't rust and enrich soil with copper trace elements as you work.

Red Pig Garden Tools

Boring, OR
redpigtools.com

Manufactured by hand with steel, fire, and an anvil, Red Pig Originals are cult favorites among gardeners who prize them as much for their U.S.-made provenance as for their usefulness.

Sneeboer & Zn

sneeboer.com

Dutch manufacturers of high-quality, hand-forged garden tools since 1913.

Featured Architects, Designers, and Landscape Architects

We are grateful to the following professionals, who contributed ideas, advice, and in many cases designs featured in the book. For our complete listing of recommended landscape architects and garden designers around the world, see the Remodelista Architect/Designer Directory at Remodelista.com.

Ben Pentreath & Associates
Bloomsbury, London
benpentreath.com

Blasen Landscape Architecture
San Anselmo, CA
blasengardens.com

Brook Landscape
Brooklyn, NY
brooklandscape.com

Bruce Bolander Architect
Los Angeles, CA
brucebolander.com

Chambers + Chambers
Mill Valley, CA
chambersandchambers.com

Commune Design
Los Angeles, CA
communedesign.com

DBA Flower Power
Wellfleet, MA
tcallis23@verizon.net

Deborah Berke Partners
New York, NY
dberke.com

Denler Hobart Gardens LLC
Ross, CA
denlerhobartgardens.com

Edible Gardens LA
Los Angeles, CA
ediblegardensla.com

Elysian Landscapes
Los Angeles, CA
elysianlandscapes.com

Feldman Architecture
San Francisco, CA
feldmanarchitecture.com

Foras Studio
Brooklyn, NY
foras-studio.com

Iain MacDonald Design
Surrey, England
iainmacdonald.co.uk

Jori Hook, Landscape Architect
Mill Valley, CA
jorihook.com

Ken Linsteadt Architects
San Francisco, CA
kenlinsteadt.com

Lindsey Taylor Garden Design
New York, NY
lindseytaylordesign.com

Machado Silvetti
Boston, MA
machado-silvetti.com

Manifold Architecture Studio
Brooklyn, NY
mani-fold.com

Margie Ruddick Landscape
New York, NY
margieruddick.com

Matthew Brown Landscape Design
Los Angeles, CA
mbrowngardens@hotmail.com

Miller Studio Landscape Architecture
Point Richmond, CA
jcmillerstudio.com

Murdock Solon Architects
New York, NY
murdocksolon.com

Rees Roberts + Partners LLC
New York, NY
reesroberts.com

Rose Uniacke
London, England
roseuniacke.com

Steven Harris Architects LLP
New York, NY
stevenharrisarchitects.com

Suzanne Shaker Inc.
New York, NY
suzanneshaker.com

Ten Eyck Landscape Architects
Austin, TX
teneyckla.com

Tom Stuart-Smith
London, England
tomstuartsmith.co.uk

Vincent Van Duysen
Knokke, Belgium
vincentvanduysen.com

WWOO
Stompetoren, Netherlands
wwoo.nl

XS Space
Brooklyn, NY
xsspace.com

Acknowledgments

This book is the result of many people's hard work, and we were very lucky to have a lavishly talented team of editors (and friends) collaborating on it. We'd like to extend thanks to the following:

Our team at Artisan: publisher Lia Ronnen and editor Bridget Monroe Itkin, for pushing us to make this book the best it could be; art director Michelle Ishay-Cohen, for transforming our ideas into something beautiful; design manager Yeon Kim and freelance designer Gordon Whiteside, for shepherding the manuscript through the design process; senior production editor Sibylle Kazeroid, for managing all the copy; production director Nancy Murray, for overseeing the book's production; and Hanh Le, for assisting with production and design. And our agent, David McCormick, who steered us to Artisan.

Our Gardenista team: Remodelista editor in chief Julie Carlson, for insisting we had to do this book (and for polishing every page), and our writers and editors, Francesca Connolly, Margot Guralnick, Justine Hand, Christine Chang Hanway, Alexa Hotz, Ellen Jenkins, Stacey Lindsay, Cheryl Locke, Jessica Marshall, Barbara Peck, Izabella Simmons, Meredith Swinehart, Lindsey Taylor, and Kendra Wilson, for contributing ideas, projects, editing skills, photo styling, and tireless support. And enormous thanks to our publisher, Josh Groves, who guided the project from start to finish and made it all seem like fun.

Our photographer: Matthew Williams, for cheerfully agreeing at least twenty times to get on just one more plane and for flying around the world to take the amazing photos that give these gardens so much life.

Finally, we would like to thank Josh Quittner for invaluable editorial advice and his magazine editor's eye (and for cooking all of us dinner so often).

Index

GARDENISTA 100 PHOTOGRAPHY CREDITS

The authors and publisher wish to thank the following for permission to reprint their illustrations in "The Gardenista 100." (Any photos not credited below are copyright © by Matthew Williams.)

Variopinte enamelware cutlery: Variopinte; Audubon Field Guide series: Best Made Co.; All Heal salve: Matter Company; French florists' bucket: Garden Trading; biergarten table: Oktoberfest Haus; bonsai scissors: Bonsai Outlet; Meriwether canvas tent: Shelter Co.; anti-fly glass sphere: Kaufmann-Mercantile; willow cloches: Williams-Sonoma; Best measuring tape: Guideboat; cast-iron fire bowl: Design Within Reach; Fermob classic bistro furniture: Fermob; Peterboro bike basket: Kaufmann-Mercantile; French outdoor thermometer: Labour and Wait; Swedish potting table: Gardenhome; Pothos houseplant: The Sill; tablecloth clamp: Manufactum; Redecker flowerpot brush: Housekeeping Store; Shaker broom: Haydenville Broomworks; Haws plant mister: Terrain; Versailles planter: Restoration Hardware; Whichford terra-cotta pot: Whichford Pottery; Steele Canvas tote bag: Steele Canvas; Sussex trug: Kaufmann-Mercantile; Dash & Albert striped outdoor rug: Annie Selke; outdoor bench: Another Country; Brommö chaise: IKEA; Odlingsvitrin miniature greenhouse: Manufactum;

Munstead flower glasses: Gertrude Jekyll Designs; Sun Valley Bronze gate latch: Source Sun Valley Bronze; Haws watering can: Haws; the Original Tree Swing: The Original Tree Swing; Dover Parkersburg galvanized tub: Great Plains Hardware; trooks: Caitlin Atkinson via Flora Grubb; English oak doorstop: Ancient Industries; butterfly chair: Steele Canvas; beeswax tea lights: Chicago Honey Co-op; Ben Wolff black clay pots: Ben Wolff Pottery; canyon lantern: Guideboat; Sun Valley bronze doorknocker: Sun Valley Bronze; Variopinte enamelware picnic plates: Variopinte; fiddle leaf fig tree: The Sill; Pawleys Island hammock: Pawleys Island Hammocks; Weber grill: Weber; twine stand: Ancient Industries; succulents: Terrain; Jackson & Perkins boot scraper: Jackson & Perkins; Hunter gardening boots: Hunter; stoneware jingle bells: Totokaelo; recycled tire trug: Atelier Home; Westport chair: Restoration Hardware; Roost hummingbird feeder: Roost Home Furnishings; olive tree topiary: Sur La Table; staghorn kokedama: The Sill; Japanese hori-hori: Garrett Wade; Casamidy lanterns: Casamidy; Labour and Wait leather work gloves: Labour and Wait; Mira copper trowel: Implementations; Kekkilä pot ladder: Finnish Design Shop; Davey & Co. bulkhead light: Guideboat; Kohler outdoor shower: Kohler; Rejuvenation classic doorbell: Rejuvenation; Henry Dean hurricane candleholder:

Kelly Ishikawa via March; Henry Dean clear glass vase: March; Aigle garden clogs: Aigle; Neutra house numbers: Jeffery Cross via Heath Ceramics; Feuerhand hurricane lantern: W. T. Kirkman Lanterns Inc.; Pointer waist apron: Pointer Brand; French enamel house numbers: Ramsign Limited; woven rattan backpack: Kaufmann-Mercantile; U.S. mailbox: Gibralter Mailboxes; Garrett Wade sharpest shovel: Garrett Wade; Eena garden tote: Canoe Online; marine light: Circa Lighting; Niwaki ladder: Niwaki; galvanized funnel: Plews & Edelmann; folding deck chair: Les Toiles du Soleil; Felco pruners: Felco USA; Alabax light: Schoolhouse Electric; Pendleton roll-up picnic blanket: Pendleton USA; striptable: The Future Perfect; Best Made axe: Best Made Co.; Great Dixter trowel: Sneeboer; Filson log carrier: Filson; coir bootscraper doormat: Wayfair; Model A Tolix chair: Design Within Reach; Campo de' Fiori aged Victorian planters: Grdn Brooklyn; lead-free garden hose: Water Right Inc.; Barn Light Electric warehouse light: Barn Light Electric; Go porch swing: Design Within Reach; Burgon & Ball herb shears: Shovel and Hoe; clay window box: Seibert & Rice; wood-handled dustpan: Brook Farm General Store; Ron Rezek ceiling fan: Y Lighting; Great States push mower: American Lawn.

Gardenista editor in chief Michelle Slatalla

Book editor Julie Carlson

Project manager Ellen Jenkins

Producers Christine Chang Hanway, Francesca Connolly, Justine Hand, Alexa Hotz, Barbara Peck, Lindsey Taylor, Megan Wilson

Text editor Barbara Peck

Writers Jessica Marshall, Barbara Peck, Jean Victor, Kendra Wilson

Stylists Alexa Hotz, Lindsey Taylor

Copy editor Meredith Swinehart

Photo research Ellen Jenkins

Intern Clementine Quittner

Library of Congress Cataloging-in-Publication Data

Names: Slatalla, Michelle, author.

Title: Gardenista / by Michelle Slatalla.

Description: New York : Artisan, [2016] | Includes index.

Identifiers: LCCN 2016012874 | ISBN 9781579656522 (hardback, paper over board)

Subjects: LCSH: Gardens—Design. | Outdoor living spaces.

Classification: LCC SB473 .S535 2016 | DDC 635—dc23 LC record available at https://lccn.loc.gov/2016012874

Art direction by Michelle Ishay-Cohen

Artisan books are available at special discounts when purchased in bulk for premiums and sales promotions as well as for fund-raising or educational use. Special editions or book excerpts also can be created to specification. For details, contact the Special Sales Director at the address below, or send an e-mail to specialmarkets@workman.com.

Published by Artisan
A division of Workman Publishing Company Co., Inc.
225 Varick Street
New York, NY 10014-4381
artisanbooks.com

Published simultaneously in Canada by Thomas Allen & Son, Limited

Printed in China

First printing, September 2016

10 9 8 7 6 5 4 3 2 1